Environmental Ethics
An Introduction for Teachers and Learners

The Env-Ethics Project has been funded with support from the European Commission. This publication reflects the views only of the authors, and the Commission cannot be held responsible for any use that may be made of the information contained therein.

ENVIRONMENTAL ETHICS

An Introduction and Learning Guide

Edited by Kees Vromans, Rainer Paslack, Gamze Yücel Isildar,
Rob de Vrind and Jürgen Walter Simon

Greenleaf
PUBLISHING

© 2012 Greenleaf Publishing Limited

Published by Greenleaf Publishing Limited
Aizlewood's Mill
Nursery Street
Sheffield S3 8GG
UK
www.greenleaf-publishing.com

Cover by LaliAbril.com
Printed in the UK on environmentally friendly, acid-free paper
from managed forests by CPI Group (UK) Ltd, Croydon, CR0 4YY

British Library Cataloguing in Publication Data:
  A catalogue record for this book is available from the British Library.

  ISBN-13: 978-1-906093-72-3 [paperback]

Authors

Kees Vromans (Hogeschool Hasdenbosch, The Netherlands)
Gamze Yücel Isildar (Gazi University, Turkey)
Rainer Paslack (Hannover Medical School, Germany)
Jürgen Simon (Hannover Medical School, Germany)
Rob de Vrind (King William I College, The Netherlands)

Further contributors

Altan Dizdar (Erbil Project Consulting Engineering, Turkey)
Elmo de Angelis (Training2000, Italy)
Kylene de Angelis (Training2000, Italy)
Daniele Nardi (Training2000, Italy)
Anouk van Butselaar (King William I College, The Netherlands)
Monika Olsson (Industrial Ecology, Royal Institute of Technology, Sweden)
Karin Edvardsson Björnberg (Royal Institute of Technology, Sweden)

Contents

List of figures and tables

Figures

Tables

Preface

As the destructive consequences of environmental problems such as global warming, water scarcity and resource and biodiversity depredation have been felt ever more heavily, people are becoming more aware of the importance of environmental protection and their own responsibilities to the environment. In recent years there has been growing interest in the behavioural components of environmental problems as human activities are increasingly recognised as the critical element in environmental degradation. The United Nations Intergovernmental Panel on Climate Change declared (IPCC 2007) that global warming has an anthropogenic source.

The number of people working in what might be termed 'environmental industries' or with environmental responsibilities in their day-to-day work has mushroomed. In many cases, however, individuals charged with protecting the environment have a set of empirical priorities: what is done, rather than moral priorities that consider what should be done. Knowledge alone does not ensure motivation to act; a value or belief system is the key in determining any action and there is a need to harmonise environmental knowledge with ethical behaviour and thus achieve behavioural change and the internalisation of environmentally ethical values.

This book, developed as part of the Env-Ethics Project,[1] an international programme to diffuse the application of environmental ethics

1 www.env-ethics.com, and see the Annex to this book.

to decision-making on pollution control, is a response to the need for a restatement of environmental ethics and for a code of behaviour and set of values that can be internalised and adopted to guide the actions of individuals involved in protecting the environment: decision-makers and environmental experts, executives and staff working in municipalities and public and government organisations throughout the EU and Turkey.

Sustainable development is given top priority as an environmental policy in most countries. It is obvious that it is very difficult to achieve sustainable development unless environmentally ethical approaches can be harmonised. It is therefore necessary to integrate ethical approaches into environmental policies. Using the book as a training manual the reader will learn how to place a value on various aspects of nature based on environmental knowledge and an understanding of environmental problems and how to harmonise those with environmental ethics. The basic facts about how natural ecosystems function and the technical dimension of environmental pollution and control practices need to be integrated with judgements on the intrinsic value of nature and our commitments to other living things and to future generations. This book will help the reader to discover a foundation for ethical standards and, more importantly, it will show how those standards can be applied to specific situations so that the reader can contribute to the prevention of environmental problems by making environmentally ethical choices.

Chapter 1 offers an introduction to the complexity of environmental ethics and environmental problems in different media, discussing scientific developments and basic philosophical background to environmental approaches to show how the relationship between people and nature that has developed over time. Chapter 2 provides a working definition of ethics and discusses the main theories of normative ethics and how moral reasoning works; it demonstrates how to describe and analyse an ethical problem and how this can be applied to the natural environment. Chapter 3 describes how the field of environmental ethics is structured in different areas and levels to which philosophical reasoning about environment and nature can be related. Chapter 4 looks at rational arguments for assigning moral status to the natural environment and shows how readers can clarify their own values in considering the environment. Chapter 5 shows how environmental issues can be regulated by laws and politics, and how environmental ethics can contribute to this task. Chapter 6 looks at sustainability and how to incorporate environmental ethics, legal principles and the 'people, profit, planet' stakeholder analysis into sustainable decision-making. The book concludes with a summary in Chapter 7 and an Annex on the pioneering work of the Env-Ethics Project.

Original case studies from different countries, with unique facts, uncertainties and circumstances, help to emphasise different perceptions of the environment and different strategies that various cultures have employed to resolve ethical dilemmas. Exercises at the end of each lesson allow readers to check that they have fully understood the information and its implications, and suggestions for further reading and resources are provided at the end to enable readers to continue the journey they have embarked on.

Ethical decision-making requires environmental knowledge (e.g. the intrinsic value of nature and knowledge of the ecosystem and how all parts of it are interconnected) and sensitivity to ethical issues. Environmental problems can be solved only if accurate technical information about the problem is supported by insights and environmental awareness. This book integrates information and ethics, bridging the gap between environmental knowledge and environmental behaviour.

1
Introduction to environmental ethics

Gamze Yücel Isildar

I would feel more optimistic about a bright future for man if he spent less time proving he can outwit Nature and more time tasting her sweetness and respecting her seniority (E.B. White).

Central goals

The reader should understand: the complexity of environmental ethics (Lesson 1) and basic environmental problems in different media (Lesson 2); scientific developments and basic philosophical background behind environmental approaches to comprehend how the relationship between human beings and nature is affected and changed in time (Lesson 3).

1.1 **Lesson 1: The complexity of environmental problems**

Objectives

On completing this lesson, the reader will understand:

- The different actors and approaches in diverse environmental cases
  - The complexity of environmental problems and variety of different solutions to these problems
  - What are the basic environmental problems (air, water, land)
  - Anthropogenic environmental pollution sources and technical prevention measures
- How and why environmental monitoring activities should be integrated with environmental ethics

Case study 1.1 **Clean and Clean Chemical Inc.**

Richard Jenkins is an environmental expert in the Ministry of Environment and Forestry in the Department of Environmental Planning and Environmental Impact Assessment. The department is in charge of drawing up and implementing regulations on environmental sites that possess ecological value and that are threatened by environmental pollution and corruption. It is also responsible for introducing measures for passing on natural heritage to later generations. Environmental experts working for the ministry are authorised to impose environmental penalties of up to €50,000 a day on facilities responsible for unlawful discharges, dumping of toxic wastes and emissions, and they have the power to order production to cease and to authorise closure of the factory. Unlike fines, which are handed down by the courts, these penalties can be imposed by Ministry of the Environment and Forestry experts within a few days of a spill or dumping.

Richard, in one of his inspections, notices that Clean and Clean Chemical Inc. is dumping hazardous wastes in an uncontrolled manner into a holding pond at the back of the factory. He knows that the toxic waste produced at the plant contains high levels of mercury. If not disposed of properly, the mercury poses a threat to nearby plants and wildlife and the people who live in the nearby community. So he speaks to the company's owner to warn him about the penalties. During the years of prosperity Clean and Clean could ignore the cost of the proper disposal of the hazardous waste generated at the facility; however, because of the slowing economy and reduced profitability of the company the owner has felt pressure to reduce expense wherever possible. Desperate to maintain profitability, he is now at the point where he is willing to sacrifice his ethics for the benefit of the 'bottom line'. He explains to Richard that with around 70 employees he has to give priority to paying their salaries and he has no extra money to pay any penalties. It appears that he is not well informed about the legislation and penalties and that he is not aware of the negative impacts and toxicity of waste produced.

Barbara, the environmental consultant of Clean and Clean, knows the importance of the situation and warning the owner is her responsibility. However, because of the economic crisis many of Barbara's clients have not used her services. Losing the Clean and Clean Chemical Inc. account at this point would be devastating to Barbara. She wonders how she can meet her customer's needs to save money on its hazardous waste disposal, while maintaining her business relationship with the company and upholding her professional code of conduct as an environmental professional.

In this situation the illegal dumping of hazardous waste might not warrant criminal actions against the company because the owner is not knowingly and willingly committing an illegal act.

The ethical dilemma at this point is what should Richard do? Should he:

- Push the owner to pay the penalty?
- Give him extra time to change his method of waste handling?
- Ignore all that he has seen?

Richard thinks about:

- How guilty he would feel if any company employees or members of the community became ill due to the illegal dumping that he chose to ignore
- How guilty he would feel if all of the company employees became unemployed if production in the company stopped (closed as a penalty)

- The harmful effects on the nearby plants, animals and people who live in the community if he chose to ignore illegal dumping
- The potential compensatory and punitive damages that the company could be forced to pay, which could drastically affect profitability
- The negative public relations that could arise and their likely effects (e.g. who wants to do business with a company that is polluting the town?)

What other examples can you add to the list of things for Richard to think about?

The second ethical dilemma is what should factory owner do? Should he:

- Pay the penalty and continue in the same manner?
- Ask for the governmental directives on the sanitary disposal of hazardous wastes?
- Offer a bribe to Richard (or to Richard's boss) to persuade him to ignore the offence?
- Dismiss the environmental consultant?

Case study 1.2 Dennis's dilemma (part 1)

Dennis is an environmental engineer working for a textile factory. His factory, like others, discharges waste-waters into a lake near a tourist area. He is responsible for the monitoring of the factory's discharges into the water and air and drawing up reports to submit to the Environment Protection Agency.

In his last monitoring, he measures that total suspended solids (TSS) and chemical oxygen demand (COD) slightly exceed the limits. The impact of this excess is not expected to be too dangerous to people in that area, but it might have an adverse effect on the fish population in the lake. To solve the problem will cost at least €100,000. It might even cost a few jobs. The factory owner thinks that the excess is a 'mere technicality' and asks Dennis to adjust the data to make it appear that the factory is in compliance.

The ethical dilemma is: what should Dennis do? He has to consider the following:

- He may lose his job
- The factory owner may offer a bribe (extra money, a new car, a better position, etc.)

- The children swimming in the lake
- Tourism activities and economic benefits in the area
- What happens if factory has to cease production?

How do you think Dennis should respond to what factory owner asks?

While the above case studies are fictional, they represent situations that almost any environmental expert could encounter. They demonstrate the peculiarity and complexity of environmental problems and the many dimensions involving social and normative implications. Sooner or later, almost everyone in the workplace is confronted by an ethical dilemma of some kind. Because of differences in organisations and in personal values and training, there may be opposing views on how these dilemmas should be resolved (Stocks and Albrecht 1993). What is clear is that we cannot afford to ignore the environment because our lives, as well as those of future generations, depend on it (Raven and Berg 2006: 2).

The goal of this book is to introduce the necessity of harmonising environmental ethics with pollution control and monitoring activities to overcome environmental problems. In this chapter, in the second part of Lesson 1, the sources, impacts and importance of environmental problems in different media (water, land, air, etc.) caused by human activities will be discussed briefly to understand the mutual relationship between humans and nature. During these discussions about the origins of environmental problems it will be beneficial to consider some basic knowledge about nature and to look at how people and nature are connected and how this relationship is mutually beneficial. What might happen if today's perception of the environment does not change? Lesson 2 will discuss chaotic environmental cases. This will help environmental experts and decision-makers to understand some of the threats facing the world in the future and the implications of not being able to foresee future issues. It will also be beneficial to take a brief look at the history of environmental development and environmentalism to be able to understand our responsibilities towards the environment. It is clear that there is no single, objective, monolithic truth about relationships between society and nature/environment. There are different truths for different groups of people in different social positions and with differing ideologies (Pepper 1996: 11). Therefore, it is necessary to understand scientific developments and at least the basic philosophical backgrounds

> We can't solve problems by using the same kind of thinking we used when we created them (Albert Einstein).

behind those ideologies or approaches to comprehend how the human–nature mutual relationship is affected and changed over time. These issues will be discussed in Lesson 3.

Figure 1.1 **Your choice?**

Look at the photographs in Figure 1.1. Which do you prefer? It is evident that environmental problems are increasing rapidly day by day and that human beings have been affected directly by those problems. The world is more crowded, more polluted, more urban, more biologically stressed and warmer than ever before in recorded history (Marsh and Grossa 2005: 1). There are encouraging signs that people are becoming aware of their responsibilities towards the environment—for example, the rise in membership of conservation and environmental organisations, public awareness campaigns, environmental policies proposed by almost all political parties. However, environmental problems still exist: the ozone layer is still depleted, biodiversity is decreasing and terrestrial land is reducing as lowlands are being covered by water. It is clear that to be an environmentalist might not be enough to protect the environment or to prevent environmental problems caused by current perceptions of nature and human–nature relations. Whatever they might profess, people do not transfer their environmental consciousness to their actions in daily life, and personal interests still outweigh the interests of the environment. This situation makes us question whether there is 'hypocrisy' or not? If there is inconsistency between environmental attitudes and actual behaviour, this will create a greater problem. In such a situation the solution of environmental problems will be more difficult than expected.

It is necessary for people, especially environmental decision-makers and experts, to harmonise and adopt ethical dimensions to the scientific, technological, economical, social and legal aspects of controlling environmental pollution to achieve real environmental protection. Fortunately, the methods of decision-making available to environmental experts (technicians) stretch from the most objective (technical) to the most subjective (ethical) (Vesilind and Morgan 2004: 467). This means that solutions to problems involving environmental changes or manipulation of environmental problems must involve not only technical engineering decisions but also other concerns such as the economic and ethical dimensions. This can be managed only by morally developed environmental experts and decision-makers. This book will discuss the need for a mechanism to change the code of behaviour and put in place a set of values that can be internalised and adopted to guide environmental professionals in their actions. That is, there is a need for effective ethical values driven by individuals in spite of the interests of capitalism. These values are different from laws by being informal and unwritten values underlying the conduct of individuals towards environment. In other words, it is very important to feel a part of nature and thus internalise ethical values.

1.1.1 Water pollution

Figure 1.2 **Polluted waters**

Water is used for nature itself, for agriculture (irrigation and live-stock supply), for drinking and personal hygiene, for transport, for energy production, for industrial production, for recreational activities (bathing or fishing), etc. It has a tremendous effect on our planet: it helps shape the continents, it moderates our climate, and it allows organisms to survive (Raven and Berg 2006: 300). As competition for this limited resource increases, its importance becomes clear. Water experts predict that more than one-third of the human population in 2025 will be unable to reach fresh water resources for drinking and other purposes. Despite this fact, we human beings continue to live with the same consumption habits, depleting and polluting these limited water resources.

Water pollution might be defined as any condition caused by human activity that adversely affects the quality of a river, lake, ocean or source of groundwater (Ray 1995: 222). As can be seen from this definition, there are two dimensions of water pollution: factors causing pollution (human activities) and water quality. Before coming to what water quality is, it will be beneficial to look at **factors causing pollution**. There are several human activities that have direct, indirect and undesirable effects on water resources. Examples are:

- Uncontrolled land use for urbanisation, industrialisation, etc.

- Uncontrolled discharge of untreated or inadequately treated wastes and leachate from landfills

- Uncontrolled and excessive use of pesticides and fertilisers

- Changes in river flow patterns (hydromorphological alterations) and their effects on sediment transportation (dams, reservoirs, etc.)

- Contamination from hazardous substances (including heavy metals, oil and microbiological toxins)

- Oil spills

- Mining

Another dimension of water pollution is **water quality**: the presence in water of impurities in such quantity and of such nature as to change physical, chemical and biological characteristics of the water and thus impair the use of the water for a stated purpose. Therefore, the definition of water quality is predicated on the intended use of the water. Water quality is assessed by monitoring to define the condition of water, to provide the basis for detecting trends and to provide information enabling the establishment of cause-and-effect relationships (Chapman 1992: 7).

Water-quality monitoring is the collection of information at set locations and at regular intervals in order to provide data that may be used to define current conditions, establish trends, etc. (Chapman 1992: 7). Due to the complexity of factors determining water quality, variations between different water sources such as lakes, rivers and groundwater or in response to human impacts might be different from source to source; there is no universally applicable monitoring standard.

The European Water Framework Directive (WFD), Directive 2000/60/EC, was adopted in 2000 as a single piece of legislation covering rivers, lakes, groundwater and transitional (estuary) and coastal waters. It requires the establishment of two primary monitoring programmes: the Surveillance Monitoring (SM) and the Operational Monitoring (OM) networks for surface waters and groundwater. However, it should be noted that this directive only defines technical points of monitoring. To understand the mechanisms of the nature itself, ecosystems, the sensitive balances between the parts of the ecosystem and its functioning are very important in the design of monitoring systems.

This book will provide a bridge both between 'environmental knowledge' and 'environmental behaviours' and between the 'technical dimension' and the 'ethical dimension' of monitoring. Environmental experts with greater awareness and sensitivity will be appreciative of their responsibilities in terms of environmental monitoring practices and in turn will display willingness for nature protection and behaviour patterns to this end.

1.1.2 Air pollution

The atmosphere is vital in maintaining life on earth. The air we breathe is necessary for life, so we expect to breathe 'clean' air. What exactly is clean air? To understand air pollution and its control, a necessary first step is to understand the composition and structure of the atmosphere. Atmosphere is a gaseous envelope surrounding the earth and comprises four important gases and other trace gases as shown in Table 1.1.

Table 1.1 **Average composition of the atmosphere in its pure form up to an altitude of 25 km**

Constant components (proportions remain the same over time and location)		**Variable components** (amounts vary over time and location)	
Nitrogen (N_2)	78.08%	Carbon dioxide (CO_2)	0.038%
Oxygen (O_2)	20.95%	Water vapour (H_2O)	0-4%
Argon (Ar)	0.93%	Methane (CH_4)	trace
Neon, Helium, Krypton	0.0001%	Sulphur dioxide (SO_2)	trace
		Ozone (O_3)	trace
		Nitrogen oxides (NO, NO_2)	trace

The two atmospheric gases most important to humans and other organisms are carbon dioxide and oxygen. Biological activities are a very important source of many atmospheric constituents. During photosynthesis, plants, algae and certain bacteria use carbon dioxide to manufacture sugars and other organic molecules; this process produces oxygen. During respiration, most organisms use oxygen to break down food molecules and supply themselves with chemical energy; this process produces carbon dioxide. Nitrogen is also important as a component of the nitrogen cycle (Raven and Berg 2006: 455). Water vapour is one of the major components of the atmosphere; it varies by volume from a trace to about 4%. Concentration changes both horizontally (how far you are from the ocean) and vertically. Water vapour absorbs infrared radiation from the sun and keeps temperature around 13 °C. Otherwise, the temperature would generally be around −18 or −19 °C. The atmosphere also has the role of blocking the surface of the earth from ultraviolet radiation and moderating the climate.

Based on the above explanation, **air pollution** can be defined as a change in the structure of atmosphere through various chemicals added from anthropogenic sources (heating systems, industrial activities, motor vehicles, etc.) or by natural events (volcanic eruptions, forest fires, etc.) in concentrations high enough to be harmful to humans, other living organisms and materials. For example, sulphur compounds emitted into the atmosphere reacting with water and other compounds in the air are converted into strong acidic compounds; reducing the pH of the rain causes acid rains. Acid rain causes considerable direct damage to buildings and monuments and indirect damage to humans. The pollutants emitted into the atmosphere must travel through the atmosphere to reach people, animals, plants or objects to have an effect (Vesilind and Morgan 2004: 303).

All air pollution problems other than global warming and ozone depletion take part in the troposphere. As can be seen from Figure 1.3, atmosphere can be divided into four main strata: troposphere, stratosphere, mesosphere and thermosphere.

The troposphere is the layer in which we live. Temperature decreases with height in this layer. In the first 5 km, where all weather conditions occur, clouds form and precipitation falls, wind blows, humidity varies from place to place and the atmosphere interacts with the surface of the earth below. Over 80% of the air is within this well-mixed layer. Pollutants do not stay for long but their concentration is high. On top

Figure 1.3 **Earth's atmosphere**

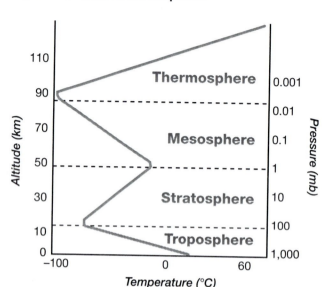

of the troposphere, in a layer called the stratosphere, the temperature profile is inverted and little mixing takes place. Pollutants can stay there for many years. The stratosphere has a high ozone concentration (90% of the total ozone concentration) and ozone absorbs the ultraviolet radiation coming from the sun. Above the stratosphere are two more layers, the mesosphere and thermosphere, which contain only about 0.1% of the air (Vesilind and Morgan 2004: 302).

Air pollution comes from many different sources: large stationary sources such as factories, power plants and smelters and smaller stationary sources such as dry cleaners and degreasing operations; mobile sources such as cars, buses, planes, lorries and trains; and naturally occurring sources such as wind-blown dust and volcanic eruptions. All these contribute to air pollution. Unfortunately, human activities make a major contribution to the air pollution as stated by the IPCC in its 4th Assessment Report: 'Global atmospheric concentrations of carbon dioxide, methane, and nitrous oxide have increased markedly as a result of human activities' (IPCC 2007).

There are many different air pollutants originating from different sources and activities. The major pollutants might be categorised according to their physical forms—particulates and gases—or according to their impact mechanisms as primary and secondary pollutants. Primary pollutants are the ones that have directly harmful impacts on living and non-living objects. Examples are carbon monoxide from car exhausts and sulphur dioxide from the combustion of coal. Further pollution can arise if primary pollutants in the atmosphere undergo chemical reactions. The resulting compounds are called secondary pollutants. Photochemical smog and acid rain are examples of these.

Particulates might be found in the air in the form of liquid and solid particles ranging considerably in size, and certain concentrations cause a variety of illnesses: asthma, lung problems, respiratory problems. When they present in the air with sulphur oxides, air visibility in the air decreases.

Major **gaseous pollutants** are nitrogen oxides, sulphur oxides, carbon oxides, ozone, hydrocarbons and oxidants. They mostly originate from the incomplete burning of fossil fuels. They are harmful to human health and materials and contribute to acid rain, etc.

The effects on health of several major air pollutants can be seen in Table 1.2.

It is clear that air pollution is very complicated problem because its sources are extensive, mixed and geographically complex in their distribution. Some air pollutants (e.g. dioxin, asbestos, toluene, and metals such as cadmium, mercury, chromium and lead compounds) are very toxic even in trace amounts and exposed to very short periods.

Air pollution prevention efforts have generally focused on both source and waste reduction. Several methods exist for removing sulphur oxides from chimneys, modification of furnaces and engines to provide more complete combustion and catalytic afterburners are just few examples to control air pollution. They are all technological solutions. However, technology might not be enough on its own. As pressures on the earth's natural systems increase, more and more people, young and old alike, are realising that environmental issues concern everyone and that they cannot be resolved by technical means only. It is understood that environmental management also rests on questions of ethics. To prevent something, the value of it should be understood well and internalised.

Table 1.2 **Effects on health of major air pollutants**

Pollutant	Source	Effects
Particulate matter (PM)	Industries, power plants, motor vehicles	• Cause of respiratory illnesses, may cause chronic conditions such as bronchitis • Heart disease • Suppression of immune system in long-term exposure
Sulphur oxides	Power plants and other industries such as petroleum refineries	• Similar to particulates • Irritation of respiratory tract (esp. together with PM)
Nitrogen oxides	Motor vehicles, industries, heavily fertilised farmlands	• Susceptibility to respiratory infections • Cause of respiratory conditions such as asthma and chronic bronchitis
Carbon monoxide	Motor vehicles, industries	• Headache and fatigue • Impairment of foetal development • Cardiovascular diseases, mental impairment or death at high levels
Ozone	Formed in atmosphere (secondary pollutant)	• Eye and throat irritation • Respiratory tract problems • Chest discomfort • Aggravation of respiratory conditions such as asthma and chronic bronchitis

1.1.3 Land pollution

Land use can be defined as the human modification of the natural environment or wilderness into cultivated fields and pastures and built environment such as settlements. Globally, humans use an estimated 38% of the world's total land area for agriculture. Another 33% of the land surface consists of urban areas and of rock, ice, tundra and desert—areas considered unsuitable for long-term human use. The remaining 29% of the land surface has natural ecosystems that are potential areas for human usage. But it should be kept in mind that lands of the earth are changing in quality and quantity. For example, global warming over the next 40–50 years will cause changes to fertile agricultural lands or aquatic environs. There is clear evidence that changing land use and land cover has significant impacts on local environmental conditions and on economic and social welfare. For example, the water cycle depends heavily on vegetation, surface characteristics, soil properties and water resources development by humans (e.g. dam construction, irrigation, channelling and wetlands drainage), which in turn affects water availability and quality. Changes in land use and land cover, climate variability and change, soil degradation and other environmental changes all interact to affect natural resources through their effects on ecosystem structure and functioning. In turn, ecological systems may respond unexpectedly when exposed to two or more perturbations (US Climate Change Strategic Program 2003: 69). Recent significant effects of land use include urban sprawl, soil erosion, soil degradation, salinisation and desertification. Problems have been exacerbated by inadequate or poorly executed land-use planning, or where legal or financial incentives have resulted in wrong decisions about land use or one-sided planning has led to over-use of natural resources for immediate production at all costs. As a consequence, the result has often been misery for large segments of the local population and the destruction of valuable ecosystems.

Improper land use should be prevented by integrated, long-term and, most importantly, holistic planning and management of land resources. To be able to manage this aim, priority should be given to the protection and sustainability of land resources instead of personal interests. Conflict of interests, as will be discussed in Lesson 2 of this chapter, is very common in the planning of land resources.

A variety of environmental problems now affect our entire world. Every environmental problem has numerous impacts on nature and human beings. The heart of the matter is that the solution to environmental problems must include an ethical dimension as well as ecological, economic, cultural and social dimensions. This is the only way to produce final, complete and successful solutions to our environmental problems.

Check your understanding of Lesson 1

1. In Case study 1.1, what do you think is the ethical dilemma facing Barbara, the environmental consultant to the factory? What should she do?

2. Give an example from your own experience (if you don't have personal experience create a scenario). Describe the different actors in that situation. How do you solve the dilemma?

3. How should the quality of drinking water differ from the quality of irrigation water?

4. How can you make a difference in conserving water in your own daily life?

5. Compare the benefits and the harm of dams and reservoirs on water resources?

6. Do you think that atmosphere is a limitless resource? Explain why?

7. Do you have any suggestions to prevent air pollution related to human behaviour?

8. How do you define the term 'ecosystem services'?

1.2 **Lesson 2: The socio-economic background and environmental responsibility**

Objectives

On completing this lesson, the reader will understand:
- The factors that make environmental problems so complex and peculiar
- The need for effective and internalised ethical values and environmental ethics as a tool
- The history of environmental development and environmentalism to be able to understand 'what lies behind' environmental attitudes and behaviours of individuals

The environment is complex and environmental issues seem sometimes to cover an unmanageable number of topics. In this lesson, some of the factors contributing to the complexity and peculiarity of the environmental problems and history of environmental approaches will be discussed.

1.2.1 Factors contributing to the complexity of environmental issues

Future technological threats

There exist some environmental issues that are only just beginning to emerge and we cannot predict their impacts on nature and on human beings in the long term (the impacts of cellular phones, endocrine disruptors, etc.). These impacts are uncertain and we might even be following weak or conflicting signals. However, they are worth tracking in any case. Although some will turn out to be irrelevant, a proportion will develop into the central issues of the future. Some issues occur suddenly and unexpectedly, so delays before science catches up may be unavoidable. Sometimes scientists look ahead and spot a problem, but do not pursue it because of competing short-term interests (Sutherland *et al*. 2008: 822). Apart from using conventional tools (such as strategic planning or risk analysis) for the prevention of unexpected results, we will have to behave ethically in consideration of unknown, suspected impacts of technological developments and discard our short -term interests.

The study of Sutherland *et al.* (2008: 821-33) highlighted 25 novel threats, which they drew up in order to give researchers the opportunity to assess environmental threats before they become a political and social problem. Examples include:

- **Nanotechnology**—although there are expected to be social benefits for medicine, electronics and the environment there is also a need to predict its impact on the environment

- **Artificially created life**—engineered organisms and synthetic microbes—could be released into the environment with unpredictable effects

- **Climate change** could bring about the spread of non-native species currently kept out by winter temperatures, damaging biodiversity and leading to the establishment of invasive communities

- **Biofuels** used as an alternative to fossil fuels has implications for the environment

- Significant **increase in coastal and offshore power generation**

Ecological crisis

An ecological crisis occurs when the environment of a species or a population changes in a way that destabilises its continued survival. There are many possible causes of such crises:

- The quality of the environment may degrade compared to species' needs, after a change in abiotic ecological factors (e.g. an increase in temperature, lower rainfalls)

- The environment may become unfavourable for the survival of a species (or a population) due to an increased pressure of predation

- The situation may become unfavourable for the quality of life of a species (or a population) because of a rise in the number of individuals (overpopulation)

Economic crisis

There might be positive or negative impacts of economic crisis on the environment. As Klare (2008) states:

> Of the many areas that will be impacted by the downturn, the environment stands out in particular. It's closely tied to the tempo of resource consumption, and significant efforts to ameliorate environmental decline will prove very expensive and out of reach for already-stretched budgets. The question thus arises: Will the crisis be good or bad for the environment, especially with respect to global warming?

Many experts believe, moreover, that demand will drop even further in the immediate future as the economic crisis deepens and consumers around the world cut back on their travel and energy use—and the less oil consumed, the less CO_2 emitted. People are staying where they are, moving closer to public transport, and flying less to second homes. This will also produce a substantial decrease in energy use and CO_2 emissions. It is unclear at this point whether the crisis will do more good or more harm to the environment.

1.2.2 Environmental responsibility

It is clear that nowadays, as people are facing the destruction of natural resources, global warming, the decrease in biodiversity, ozone-layer depletion, accelerated rates of land degradation and desertification, they have begun to feel the consequences of these problems deeply and are convinced that the environment is growing worse. Because of this, environmental perceptions have changed and developed from the mid-20th century to today. The number of people who are interested in environmental issues has increased and being 'environmentalist' has become fashionable at many levels of society in Europe and around the world. Conservation organisations and environmental non-governmental organisations (NGOs) are registering more members, public awareness campaigns abound, environmental policies appear in the manifestos of almost all political parties, decision-makers have enacted legislation on environmental issues and the Nobel Peace Prize 2007 was awarded jointly to the Intergovernmental Panel on Climate Change (IPCC) and former US vice-president Al Gore for their work in disseminating knowledge about human-made climate change. These changes seem to indicate that people are becoming more aware of the importance of nature and thus their own responsibilities to the environment. It might therefore be expected that environmental consciousness will increase and attitudes towards the environment change, resulting in changes in behaviour towards environmental protection. However, numerous studies that have examined environmental attitudes (e.g. Ewert and Galloway 2004: 58; Olli, Grendstadt and Wollebaek 2001: 181) report that a paradox arises when actual behaviour is compared to expressed beliefs and attitudes. That is, people do not incorporate these changes in attitudes, perception and environmental consciousness into their daily lives and do not live in an environmentally friendly way; they do not change their consumption habits, and they do not take care of environmental values in their relations with each other and with nature. There is a conflict between personal interest and the protection of nature. Therefore this dilemma certainly requires discussion on the need for a mechanism to change the code of behaviour and produce a set of values that are internalised and adopted to guide their actions by the individuals. That is, there is a need for effective ethical values driven by individuals in spite of the interests of world capitalism. These values are informal and unwritten, based on the conscience of individuals. In other words, internalised ethical values are necessary to make individuals behave in a genuinely environmentally friendly way by feeling themselves to be part of the environment and feeling nature inside themselves.

The **moral development of individuals** means that individuals form their own ethical framework to live in harmony with nature by assessing the consequences of their relationship with nature. We each have a capacity to change our relationship with nature as soon as we notice or are faced with the adverse impacts of existing interactions and to move towards a rehabilitated, cleaner environment. We should reconsider our relations with nature as well as our capacity to destroy nature. On the one hand, human beings tend to overuse natural resources, assuming they are limitless; but at the same time, they also have the capacity to prevent pollution and destruction through technology and their own ethical values (Tekeli 2000). They have the freedom to choose the direction they want to go in: to destroy or to protect. Freedom offers different choices. What is needed to make the right choice of the most appropriate alternative that fits our personality, culture, religion and desires is knowledge. Knowledge will help us to determine where the border lies between our freedom and the freedom of others, including nature. The choices we make are good indicators of our ethical approach. We can use conscience to decide what is bad or what is good and where our responsibilities lie, and act accordingly. In fact there is a close connection between ethics and responsibility. As individuals, we have **responsibilities towards nature** (to guarantee the sustainability of natural resources or to try to re-establish damaged balances or rehabilitate ecosystems, etc.), **towards society** (we are living in society and have to consider the common interests; however, those interests should not be only human-centred) and **towards future generations.**

If the 'wholeness' of the ecosystem or the fragility and sensitivity of nature are well understood by us as individuals and we each can conceive our position within nature, we reach a state of consciousness. Scientific knowledge and experience of nature increase sensitivity and may lead to an enhanced consciousness that leads to a sense of responsibility. This framework lays the foundations for concepts of good and bad, and by experiencing the good and the bad we can deduce our responsibilities, which help us to achieve 'good' in the context of internalised environmental ethics. In the light of these discussions, individuals' relationship with nature—their dual-sided capacity to destroy or to protect—and how they can harmonise responsibilities with actions are important problem areas that should be looked at.

Check your understanding of Lesson 2

1. Give examples of factors that might have unexpected or unpredictable effects on nature
2. What do you think about unexpected consequences of technology on the function of ecosystems?

1.3 **Lesson 3: The history of environmentalism**

Objectives

On completing this lesson, the reader will be able to understand:
- How the people–nature relationship developed over time
- The impacts of social and economic developments on environmental history

Since ancient times, different approaches and ideas have been developed on the relationship between humans and nature. Early people spent their entire existence trying to meet their basic needs such as food and shelter. They had limited impacts on nature. However, when farming and hunting advanced, small interferences to nature began. Over time, as society developed, understanding of what might be considered of basic needs changed to encompass more food, better shelter, etc., and so human beings overused nature to meet their expectations and for their self-interest, causing natural resources to be depleted and polluted. With the onset of the industrial revolution in Europe in the 17th and 18th centuries, a revolutionary paradigm defending nature as a resource to be exploited by people to improve their living standards made humankind become increasingly dominant and people feel that they were the masters of the universe. Since then people have behaved accordingly and it is now recognised that ecological and environmental problems are the cumulative product of this paradigm.

The first meaningful studies in environmental science began to appear in the last quarter of the 18th century. George Louis Leclerc published *Historie Naturel* (*History of Nature*) in 36 volumes between 1749 and 1788. In these books, since they belonged to pre-industrial period, the destructive role of humankind is not recognised and it seems that humankind lives in harmony with nature. However, in the same period, Thomas Malthus (1766–1834) noticed the negative impacts of an uncontrolled increase in population and he was as pessimistic as contemporary environmentalists about the future.

Malthus established the basis of a 'limits to growth' approach. In the light of Malthus's ideas, many others, from Adam Smith to Garrett Hardin, have studied the impact of uncontrolled population increase on nature.

At the beginning of the 19th century geographers such as Ritter and Von Humboldt were interested in the interaction between humans and nature, too. In Ritter's analysis the mutual relationship between humans and nature occurred on a regional basis and was determined by theological conditions, whereas Von Humboldt gave priority to the natural sciences and the mutuality of the human–nature relationship itself. During this period those people come to the point of 'environmental determinism' in which natural conditions have more effect than social determinants on the evolution of living things. As an important representative of environmental determinism, Charles Darwin (1809–1882) can be regarded as landmark figure (Pepper 1996) in environmental history. He identified the environment as a force shaping plant and animal physiology and behaviour and postulated the theory of competition among animals as a mechanism for enhancing species' chances of survival. While discussing the history of environmentalism, Darwin's evolutionary theory should also be mentioned. According to this theory, variations occurred between individuals in a species substantially by chance. Hence, individuals who had features that were best adapted to the environment (i.e. 'fittest') were more likely to survive than those that were poorly adapted. There is a struggle for resources and competition between individuals to be the 'fittest'. In the long run, this competition and struggle between species is so nicely balanced that nature remains uniform. In this aspect of his theory there is an idea of systems in dynamic equilibrium that is very important for our discussions on human–nature relationships: the transition from (homocentric) anthropocentric to ecocentric approaches.

During this period, the contribution of human beings to environmental problems began to be discussed more frequently with the realisation that humans were not as innocent as had been thought. For example, the American conservationist George Perkins Marsh emphasised the destructive impacts of human beings on nature in *Man and Nature* in 1864 (a revised edition was published in 1874 titled *The Earth as Modified by Human Action: Man and Nature*.) At the same time, Haeckel, a German biologist and naturalist, whose thoughts ran parallel to Darwin's, developed a concept of 'ecology' and defined it as 'the study of the reciprocal relations between living organisms and biotic and abiotic environment' (*Mammal Species of the World*, 1866). By this definition there is a call for holistic thinking, recognising the full implications of our place in the global ecosystem, where whatever we do to one part of that system will affect all the other parts (Pepper 1996), as opposed to individualism, advocated by the mechanistic approaches that were much more common at that time.

Meanwhile, other nature writers such as Henry David Thoreau (1817–1862) and John Muir (1838–1914) were talking in terms of 'respect for nature' and emphasising the importance of land. Although they met opposition from the outset from those with economic interests to protect, such as timber companies and politicians, they argued that valuable and unique areas should be protected. Inspired by Thoreau and Muir and other naturalists, environmental awareness began to spread through the Western world. National parks were declared in Australia, New Zealand and Canada, and the United Kingdom began to establish its first conservation-based organisations such as the Royal Society for the Protection of Birds in 1893 and the National Trust in 1894.

Like Thoreau and Muir, Aldo Leopold (1887–1948) was thinking wildernesses were spiritual places and their loss meant a spiritual loss to humanity. He made an important contribution to the development of the idea that 'man is not a master of the universe, only one of the parts of nature' and he established a connection with 'ethics' in the nature–human relationship. He believed humans should extend to nature the same ethical sense of responsibility that we extend to each other. His famous essay, 'The Land Ethic' (published posthumously in 1949) in particular provided a foundation for ecocentric approaches. In it, he claimed 'something is right when it tends to preserve the integrity, stability and beauty of the biotic community. It is wrong when it tends otherwise' (Leopold, 1949). Merchant (1992) calls this the first formulation of modern ecocentric ethics, which is another subclass of environmental approaches based on environmental ethics.

Within 100 years a small number of concerned people had tried to raise environmental awareness in the world. However, until the 1960s that concern for the environment was not turned into an organised movement. Much of the literature agrees that the milestone marking the birth of the environmental movement was Rachel Carson's book *Silent Spring*, published in 1962. *Silent Spring* describes the slow but absolute poisoning of the environment by pesticides and by DDT in particular. The message in the title is clear: one day there will be a spring without life. She described in detail how chemicals such as the insecticide DDT enter the food chain and accumulate in the fatty tissues of animals, including humans, and can result in cancer. Although she was criticised and the chemical industry tried to ban the book, when investigations were made she was found to be correct, leading to the banning of DDT and the scrutiny of the effects of other chemicals. This development was very important since it scientifically proved that the environment was being damaged by humans. Previously, environmental problems had been the concern of just a few people, but with this publication people understood that their own lives were at risk and environmental issues could no longer be ignored. It is therefore possible to claim that the ecological movement was born with Rachel Carson's *Silent Spring*.

Ecologist Garrett Hardin argued in his article 'The Tragedy of the Commons', first published in 1968, that, given an ecosystem open to all, if individuals use natural resources only for their own interests ultimately those resources become degraded to the detriment of everyone (Hardin 1968). The herders in his example treat the environment as a 'free' set of goods and services (Pepper 1996: 56). His much-debated article 'Living on a Lifeboat' argued that aiding poor countries causes population increase resulting in environmental degradation and human suffering (Hardin 1974). Biologist Paul R. Ehrlich (1968) warned people of the possibility of unavoidable disaster if population growth was not taken under control, echoing the Malthusian approach.

These discussions are important since their widest reflections could be seen in the emergence of the Club of Rome, a global think-tank of people from academia, civil society, diplomacy and industry founded in 1968. Its first report, *The Limits to Growth* (Meadows *et al.* 1972), described the consequences of natural resource depletion. The report gives different scenarios by model analysis of five variables— technology, population, nutrition, natural resources and energy— focusing on the limited nature of natural resources, and describes how population growth rate will be affected if production and consumption patterns do not change. Although *The Limits to Growth* has been heavily criticised, it publicised for the first time the idea that development should be in balance with the finite size of the earth's resources.

As a result of a rapid increase in environmental problems, and stimulated by the intellectual findings of the Club of Rome, the United Nations Conference on the Human Environment met in Stockholm in June 1972. This was the first event that turned the environment into a major issue at the international level. The conference drew together both developed and developing countries, considering the need for a common outlook and for common principles to inspire and guide the peoples of the world in the preservation and enhancement of the human environment. As stated in the Declaration of the Conference,

> Local and national governments have to bear the greatest burden for large-scale environmental policy and action within their jurisdictions. International cooperation is also needed in order to raise resources to support the developing countries in carrying out their responsibilities in this field. A growing class of environmental problems, because they are regional or global in extent or because they affect the common international realm, will require extensive cooperation among nations and action by international organisations in the common interest. The Conference calls on governments and peoples to exert common efforts for the preservation and improvement of the human environment, for the benefit of all people and for their posterity.[1]

With the establishment of NGOs, especially dealing with environmental issues, new social movements emerged in those years. Environmentalism began to define its own problematic areas. From then

1   United Nations Environment Programme; www.unep.org/Documents. Multilingual/Default.asp?documentid=97&articleid=1503, accessed 25 March 2012.

on, the necessity of environmental protection and improvement, the prevention of environmental problems and the value of nature were accepted by many people in different positions and in different countries. There was a great deal of concern over nuclear weapons and nuclear power in the 1960s. In response, more radical environmental pressure groups such as Greenpeace and Friends of Earth were established at the end of the 1960s and in the early 1970s, and began taking direct action against environmental destruction. Such movements by a wide array of these types of NGO have been one of the factors in shaping public awareness about environmental problems.

Environmental movements were followed by the inclusion of eco-centric approaches in party politics such as the mayoral election in France in 1977 when three ecological groups formed the Collectif Ecologie '78 for the purpose of campaigning for the parliamentary elections (Simonnet 1982). Political activists advocated the formation of 'green' parties that would rewrite the social and political agenda to include policies on saving other species and protecting nature and human health. This encouraged environmentalists and the politicisation of environmental movements have been observed in some countries in Europe, such as the red–green coalitions (of socialists/social democrats and environmentalists) in Germany and elsewhere.

These trends found many supporters around the world especially from among the young and intellectuals. And through their contradictory ideas, these social movements led to the development of new areas in geographical arena—humanist, radical, anarchist, phenomenological, etc.—and all these areas have different paradigms, and thus different environmental perspectives (Tekeli 2000: 3).

In the 1970s, there was a widespread belief that environmental problems were caused by scientific and technological progress. In the 1980s, it became obvious that environmental problems were more related to society and societal occurrences than to science and technology alone. The defining political events of the 1980s were the breakdown of the Eastern bloc and the end of the polarisation between Western and Communist countries and their allies in the developing world. The situation was different in the developing countries that registered little growth in income. Dealing with the cycle of poverty became a particular challenge as population growth in the developing world not only continued but an increasing number of the poor were living in cities. The number of refugees doubled. As urban populations grew, cities were unable to cope with their physical infrastructural demand. And in the 1980s a range of catastrophic events (the Chernobyl nuclear power plant explosion, the oil spill from the *Exxon Valdez* supertanker, etc.) left permanent impacts on the environment and human health. This situation led to the birth of the idea that environmental issues are systemic and addressing them requires long-term strategies, integrated action and the participation of all countries and all members of society.

Communicating the message that environment and development were interdependent required a process that carried authority and credibility for both the North and the South, for government and the business sector, and for international organisations and civil society. This was reflected by the report of the United Nations World Commission on Environment and Development called *Our Common Future* (WCED 1987), which was another important landmark in this discussion. The report analysed the relationship between environmental degradation and the economy on a worldwide scale. Public meetings were held in both developed and developing regions, and the process empowered different groups to articulate their views on issues such as agriculture, forestry, water, energy, technology transfer and sustainable development in general. The term **sustainable development** became a new watchword, defined as development that meets the needs of the present without compromising the ability of future generations to meet their own needs.

The WCED identified the new and threatening environmental problems as global warming and ozone-layer depletion and concluded that existing decision-making structures and institutional arrangements, at both international and national levels, could not cope with the demands of sustainable development. Thus it would be necessary to strengthen the non-governmental sector with the formation of many new organisations to engage in the field of environment and development. It might be said that there was another paradigmatic shift from ecocentrism to homocentrism, which falls between the two extremes of the egocentric and the ecocentric approaches.

A second conference, the Earth Summit in Rio, in which the new concept of sustainability became more dominant and was discussed by a wider range of people from different sectors, was held in 1992 to decide what should be done for the worldwide application of sustainable development principles. The Earth Summit emphasised the link between environmental problems and economic and social justice issues. The world leaders agreed to combat global warming, protect biodiversity and stop using dangerous chemicals. These intentions have been executed with varying degrees of success.

For example, although many nations signed up to the Kyoto Protocol, introduced at Rio, aiming to cut down carbon dioxide emissions to prevent global warming, some developed countries gave first priority to their own short-term interests. Countries with an economy dependent on oil, such as the USA and Saudi Arabia, declined to be a party to the protocol and, especially in the case of the USA, began a tradition of refusing to commit to anything binding on carbon emissions.

Ten years after the Earth Summit in Rio, the Johannesburg Earth Summit was held in 2002 aiming to evaluate the implementation of strategies for sustainable development that had been determined in Rio. More concrete decisions were taken, such as to halve the number of people in the world who lacked basic sanitation by 2015. Five problem areas were identified: water and sanitation; energy; health; agriculture; and biodiversity. Although developed countries (European Union countries and the USA) had been dominant in the previous summits, by the time of Johannesburg the developing countries were becoming increasingly aware of environmental issues, the unequal distribution of natural resources and the contribution of developed countries to environmental pollution, and they therefore pressed more strongly for their interests to be given greater consideration. However, as in Rio, some of the developed countries' corporate interests hijacked the agenda: the USA, Japan and the oil-producing countries once again discouraged the promotion of renewable energy resources in order to favour their own economic interests.

In the light of the above brief history, basic assumptions of a common environmental world-view reached globally today could be summarised as follows:

- Destructive impacts of environmental problems have begun to be felt heavily in developed countries as well as in developing countries

- Individuals in contemporary societies have certain levels of environmental awareness and knowledge. Therefore changes in their perception and attitudes are expected

- Basic environmental policies have been introduced, such as the rational use of natural resources, for the benefit of present and future generations

- Sustainable development has became the new paradigm

- And finally it is the time for action!

What is meant by 'it is the time for action' should be emphasised further. It is clear that even now not enough has changed. More and more people accept that environmental problems are caused by humans and that the environment should be protected by humans and from humans. However, even after 150 years it is still not agreed whether the environment should be protected because it is a source of food, energy and other materials we need, or because it has value in its own right. Now, more than ever, it is important to recognise the critical crossroads we are at.

To summarise this section: in the mechanistic world-view created during the 17th century, scientific revolution constructs the world as a machine made up of interchangeable atomic parts that are manipulated by humans. This approach and its ethical legitimate use of nature as a commodity and instrumental good serves the welfare of human beings. Mechanical thinking and industrial capitalism lie at the root of many environmental problems. However, this mechanistic world-view, which is the product of early capitalism, is replaced, as the world begins to experience environmental problems, by an eco-centric world-view that is holistic and emphasises the importance of the whole over the parts and does not separate humans from the environment. This ecological paradigm entails a new ethic in which all parts of the ecosystem, including humans, are of equal value and recognises the intrinsic value of all beings. It pushes social and ecological systems towards new patterns of production, reproduction, and consciousness that will improve the quality of human life and nature.

Check your understanding of Lesson 3

1. Describe a particular environmental problem and discuss individuals' relationship with nature—their dual-sided capacity to destroy or to protect nature in your specific scenario. Include the results, impacts on nature, etc.
2. Give examples from your daily life of your own environmentally friendly behaviour
3. How would you increase environmental awareness and recognition of our responsibilities towards nature?
4. What do you think will happen to the life-span of the earth if consumptive habits remain constant?
5. Give an example of the impact of different cultures on environmental approaches

2
Ethics
The search for decision criteria

Kees Vromans

Central goals

The reader should: understand a working definition of ethics, the three main theories, the meaning of norm and value and how correct moral reasoning works (Lesson 1); be able to describe, analyse and assess a moral problem and justify the response (Lesson 2); and understand how ethics apply to the natural environment (Lesson 3).[1]

1 Chapters 2 and 4 are based on the lectures of the Department of Environmental Studies of HAS Den Bosch, University of Applied Sciences. Since the early 1990s environmental ethics has become a niche in the academic world, especially at the University of Amsterdam. The Amsterdam School can be seen as being in the forefront of a radical first wave of environmental ethics. In the lectures at the Department of Environmental Science the main goal of environmental philosophical analysis as serving the solution of environmental problems meets this first wave. The main goal of ethics is to clarify values, and students are given tools to find out what their end-values are. They are induced to say what their values are on topics of environment and sustainable development and confront their values with the ideas of instrumental and intrinsic value and of basic attitudes of humans towards nature and environment. Practical moral dilemmas are analysed, discussed and solved using a range of tools. Environmental ethics becomes part of what one of the students calls 'a never-ending journey'.

2.1 **Lesson 1: Towards a working definition of ethics**

Prescribing a placebo

In interviews doctors and other people working in the medical sector are confronted with the question of whether or not it is good to prescribe a placebo.

One doctor argues that some of his patients aren't satisfied until he prescribes something. So to calm the patient he prescribes a placebo. It is not convenient for him if the patient keeps on asking for a prescription and it is a lot easier to prescribe a placebo.

The interviewer asks why he prescribes a placebo. The doctor says he wants to help the patient. He wants to cure. The interviewer asks what the doctor says when the patient asks what kind of medicine he has prescribed. The doctor says that the medicine contains such-and-such that will help the patient to recover.

The interviewer asks whether he isn't deceiving his patients. Shouldn't he always tell the truth? The doctor sees no problem because he is helping the patient. The interviewer asks what he does when the patient wants more of the same because the medicine is 'curing' him. The doctor says he prescribes more of the same placebo. He isn't doing the patient any harm.

The interviewer asks another doctor what is in the placebo. She replies that it is 'nothing'. Asked whether the patient has to pay, the doctor argues that to achieve the effect of a cure, you have to ask the patient to pay. If you say the patient doesn't have to pay because there is 'nothing' in the medicine, the prescription of the placebo has no effect.

There are many kinds of problems: social, economic, psychological and ecological.

Sometimes we know instinctively that we are dealing with an ethical problem or a moral dilemma, but not always. To fully understand what kinds of problem are ethical, we have to learn more about ethics and philosophy.

In Lesson 1 we first look at the history of Greek philosophy to find the roots of ethics. By comparing ethics with other disciplines we see that ethical thinking is a special way of viewing the world and from this comparison we compose a working definition of ethics. That definition leads us to one of three kinds of ethics: the normative. Normative ethics are all to do with moral argument, with clarifying our values.

There are two kinds of value and three kinds of ethical theory. They can be a tool to help us in our moral arguments.

As we become more aware of ethical theory we start to identify more moral dilemmas and ethical problems. We can find them in the newspaper, on television and in our daily conversations.

2.1.1 A working definition of ethics

The word 'philosophy' stems from the Greek words *phileîn*, 'to love', and *sophía*, 'wisdom'. So philosophers love wisdom; they are looking for wisdom or truth. According to some philosophers, philosophy starts with wondering, with a question. The earliest philosophers were philosophers of nature. The history of Greek philosophy starts with Thales of Miletus.

After the philosophy of nature comes metaphysics. The Greek *meta* means 'over' but it can also be understood as 'beyond' or 'after'. The first editors of Aristotle called his works on philosophy metaphysics because they followed on from, or went beyond, his physical investigations. It is likely that the term won ready acceptance as denoting the part of philosophy that reaches beyond nature (*physis*) to discover the 'true nature' of things, their ultimate essence and the reason for being.

Aristotle was the first to make a serious and systematic study of moral principles, which he called 'ethics'. So ethics is also a part of Greek philosophy.

Figure 2.1 *Scuola di Atene (School of Athens)* by Raphael

Note: In one of Raphael's most famous frescoes, commissioned for the Apostolic Palace in the Vatican, Plato (pointing up) and Aristotle (with palm facing down) are the two central figures surrounded by a multitude of other philosophers.

The Greek called the resolution of theoretical problems by systematic and reasonable thinking 'philosophy'.

There are many definitions of ethics. Here we will be satisfied with a working definition that can be used to question the human actions that are so significant to applied studies. In ethics people think about their actions. They ask what is right or wrong. A **definition of ethics** is:

> Systematic thinking
> about the action
> of humans,
> asking the question
> whether that action is good or not good

The question of whether human action is good or not good can be applied to all kinds of disciplines, such as the economic, the social and the psychological. They all hold certain values. Ask yourself what the values of economics are. Next, the values of someone who is involved in the law. Next, the values of someone who is doing social studies. (You can add other disciplines.) The result is a list of values. And, as you can see, it is a list of **conflicting** values.

What is special about ethics? Is ethics a special way to view reality? The aim of ethics is to achieve the ultimate good, the **end-value**. Ethics arises when values of other disciplines, any values at all, are conflicting. Ethical questions are asked when there is a conflict of values and to choose between them becomes a problem. At that moment I am confronted with the question: What ought I to do? Which value is the most important, is good, **in the end**?[2] The conflict of values brings us back to the working definition of ethics:

Systematic thinking
about the action
of humans,
asking the question
whether that action is good/not good
in the end.

2.1.2 Three kinds of ethics

We can distinguish three kinds of ethics:

1. **Descriptive ethics.** This kind of ethics describes what people actually do, how people think or have thought about good and not good. It describes facts. Descriptive ethics can be found within anthropology, history and psychology

---

2 In this book the expression 'in the end' is based on a view that the scope of ethics has to do with 'intrinsic good'. So we are looking for the end-value. What do you consider is the most important value among the values that are at stake in a particular situation? Which value guides your action? The expression 'in the end' has a connotation of utilitarian ethics, which, as we see later, finds the answer to the question in the definition through weighing the consequences of human action. But it is also possible that your ethical, moral conclusion has to do with the Greek *deon*, duty, to act according to principles, or with a virtue such as charity.

2. **Normative ethics.** This kind of ethics tries to figure out what people *ought* to do. It is a rational attempt to decide what are the limits to human action, what are the norms for human action and what are the values humans are pursuing or ought to pursue. Normative ethics are action-guiding or prescriptive. Normative ethics are dealt with in the scenario on placebos above where participants are invited to clarify their values and are willing to discuss them

3. **Metaethics.** This is the analytical, critical thinking about normative ethics. Metaethics tries to answer questions such as: 'What do normative theories *mean* by "good" and "right"?' and 'What does "value" mean?'

2.1.3 The theories of normative ethics

When you are dealing with **normative ethics**, you try to find out what people ought to do, what the limits to the action of humans are (norms) and what they ought to pursue (values). Studying normative ethics leads to three main theories or groups of theory. Each group has its own arguments to identify human action as good or not good. Two of the main theories are **teleological** and **deontological**. Some philosophers insist on adding a third one: **virtue** ethics.

Teleological theories

These theories cover moral judgement that emphasises the effect, the result and the consequences of human action. They can be called the theories of **consequentialism**.

The term 'teleological' is derived from the Greek *telos*, meaning 'goal'. As a short cut one could talk about goal ethics. One teleological theory is utilitarianism. **Utilitarianism** identifies the criterion for the good or not good nature of a human action as the benefit or the harm caused by that action. A 'good' action should benefit not only the actor but also other people involved. An important question is: who is involved in a particular action? When the action benefits the majority of the people involved, the action is good. When the action harms the majority, it is not good.

John Stuart Mill lived in England in the age of industrialisation. The British Empire 'ruled the waves' but the situation of the labouring classes was very bad. They had no proper housing, no health-care, and no education. Mill was in favour of the 'enlightenment' of the labourers. Can you give the arguments for his position by using utilitarian reasoning? Just think of 'the greatest happiness for the greatest number'.

John Stuart Mill

To the founding father of utilitarianism, the English philosopher and reformer Jeremy Bentham (1748–1832), benefit and harm equate to pleasure and pain. They guide the actions of humans. His individualistic theory is that an action should produce the greatest happiness for the greatest number. He thought that, before deciding what we ought to do, we have to consider the possible consequences of our action. We ought to do what generates the most pleasure. We have to apply this to every single action. His theory is therefore called act-utilitarianism.

Bentham's follower John Stuart Mill (1806–1873) was an advocate of a more social utilitarianism. Every individual ought to help in achieving the greatest happiness for the greatest number, not by looking at every single act but by acting according to a rule. A rule that—in practice—has shown to generate the most pleasure. The theory of Mill is therefore called rule-utilitarianism.

Deontological theories

This group of theories don't put the accent on the consequences in the moral judgement of human actions. They don't deal with the goal of the actions. They ask what the norm is. The ethical question 'what ought I to do?' is judged by the intention of the actor, by what he or she considers to be his or her duty. The Greek word for duty is *deon*.

Deontological philosophers argue that an action is right if it is executed according to a principle or norm. The only thing that is right is good will and intention. The nature of our motives and intentions is important. The German philosopher Immanuel Kant (1724–1804) can be seen as the godfather of deontology. According to Kant we learn what good will is when we are confronted with duty. Kant argues that moral rules precede actions. He calls those moral duties 'maxims'. A maxim is a rule of life: a demand, a norm, a principle or a duty. An action is morally right when the action is based

Immanuel Kant

on a valid moral rule. To verify whether that rule of life—and the action—is morally valid, Kant offers a criterion. He argues that we have to universalise the rule of life. We know what our duty is when we ask ourselves the question 'Do I want everybody to act in the same way that I intend to act now under these circumstances?' Thus Kant's categorical imperative is born: act only according to the maxim that you want to be a universal law. A hypothetical imperative commands action in a given circumstance. A categorical imperative, denotes 'an absolute, unconditional requirement that asserts its authority in all circumstances, both required and justified as an end in itself'.[3]

Next Kant tries to prove that such a universal law exists. To show there is a universal law that can exist apart from our goals, detached from consequences, he has to prove that there are goals that are an end in themselves. According to Kant 'each human is an end in himself'. The human being is intrinsically good. Now he offers a new formulation of the categorical imperative: 'Act in such a way that humanity both in your own person as in every other person is considered to be an end and not a mere tool' (*Foundations of the Metaphysics of Morals*, 1785).

To Kant a rule of life or maxim is valid if it survives the proof of the categorical imperative. If the principle can be considered a universal

3 en. wikipedia. org/wiki/Categorical_imperative, accessed 20 March 2012.

law and doesn't offend human dignity, either your own or that of anybody else, then it is a morally valid principle. An action according to that principle is morally right.

Virtue ethics

Virtue ethics is considered by some philosophers to be the third major approach in normative ethics. It may be identified as the approach that emphasises virtue, or moral character, in contrast to deontology, which emphasises duties or rules, or teleology, which emphasises the consequences of actions (consequentialism). So, in order to call a human action good or not good, you look to virtue: an action is right only if it is an action that a virtuous person would perform in the same circumstances.

Virtue ethics has a strong commitment to 'human flourishing', and the highest human good (which Aristotle called *eudaimonia*) is reached, both for a person and society, by practising virtues. A virtue is a moral characteristic that a person needs to live well: for example, charity (see Fig. 2.2), and virtue ethics assumes that there is a universal set of virtues that all humans should live by. But different lists of virtues have been drawn up throughout history and they may differ from one society to another.

Figure 2.2 *Charity* **by Peter Brueghel the Elder**

Note: One of a series of the Seven Virtues, drawings made by Brueghel the Elder for publication as prints c. 1559.

2.1.4 Norm and value

In the book we use the terms 'norm' and 'value'. A **norm (or rule)** prescribes what we ought or ought not to do in a particular situation. A **value** is something that we consider to be good and that we want to strive after.

Kant gives hardly any examples of norms. He has only a formal explanation of how to arrive from your own 'maxim' to a universal rule. For examples of rules we can look at history and religion: for instance, the Ten Commandments of the Old Testament or even the wisdom of the Native American, Chief Seattle. Another example of a set of rules is the United Nations Universal Declaration of Human Rights.[4]

According to Van Willigenburg *et al.* (1993), it is possible to distinguish a number of general moral rules ('principles') within ethics for the public domain that give expression to what is normative for a society of humans:

- **Do no harm**

- **Do good**

- **Respect autonomy**. Respect the self and the uniqueness of every human

- **Be just.** Equal treatment of others and a fair distribution of pleasure and pain

We can distinguish relational, professional and public norms. We should also be aware of consequentialist and deontological rules. The first means that you are basing your moral judgement on the consequences of your action and you are acting correctly when the good consequences of your action overweigh the bad ones. The second means that you ought to act according to a norm regardless of the consequences.

Here we concentrate on learning about value as used in the terms 'functional or instrumental value' and 'intrinsic value':

4 www.un.org/en/documents/udhr.

- **Functional or instrumental value.** Something has value—is good— because one sees it as an instrument, a tool to realise one's goals or ends. It is especially useful in economics.

- **Intrinsic value.** This value is an end in itself. It isn't a mere instrument to something else; money, for example, is only good because it is an instrument to other values. Only to the miser does money have intrinsic value. Intrinsic value is a value regardless of any direct usefulness to human beings

Ask yourself what happens when you attribute either instrumental or intrinsic value to other living beings and to elements of nature. What does that mean regarding your actions towards those living beings and to those elements of nature? In environmental ethics those values and the basic attitudes of humans towards nature are the central theme.

Human actions also can be judged to be intrinsically or instrumentally good. Deontological actions are good because they are good in themselves or they are wrong because they are wrong in themselves. They don't need any further justification. To the utilitarians actions are right so far as they bring 'happiness' to the largest group of people involved. Is the action useful to most of the people involved and therefore good/right or causing harm and therefore morally wrong?

2.1.5 Correct moral reasoning

What is the problem when moral, ethical discussions last forever and never come to a consensus or common conclusion? It seems likely that something goes wrong with moral reasoning and argument. It looks easy when you see correct moral reasoning shown as the following formula.

1. The moral, ethical presupposition

+

2. The facts

_____

3. The moral, ethical conclusion

Take the following example. In the classroom I ask the students whether they think that they ought to act according to (legal) rules in every situation.

a. Some of them say that everybody has to act according to (legal) rules in every situation

b. Some say that there are exceptions. One of the exceptions is an emergency situation. When there is an emergency situation you are allowed to break the rules

I confront them with the following situation: a team of journalists are making a daily TV programme on current issues. One of the issues is: do the people who make the laws act according to those laws? The reporters are following Dutch ministers to show how they act. During the start of the war in Iraq, all ministers have to come to The Hague as quickly as possible for an emergency meeting. One of the ministers is on a visit in the east of the Netherlands, about 200 kilometres from The Hague. On the way to The Hague the driver of the minister's car exceeds the speed limit several times. The TV reporters are following that car, record the incidents and broadcast them the same evening. The students holding opinion (a) conclude that the action is not good, wrong. The students holding opinion (b) conclude that the action is good, right.

So do you still think ethical reasoning is easy? What goes wrong?

In moral discussions participants don't make explicit what their presupposition is (see [1] in the formula). What do they value in a particular situation; what is the principle, the norm, the rule?

Very often participants present facts as values. The participants have to agree on the facts in a particular situation (see [2] in the formula). It is best to know the facts, but when you don't know them you have to tell each other what you think are the facts. Then you can have a discussion about values.

Sometimes participants make a connection between (1) and (2). In the example, the expression 'emergency situation' has been used. You should make explicit what you consider to be an emergency situation. If not, your conclusion can differ from that of someone else. When you consider an emergency is a matter of life and death and someone else considers being on time at an important meeting as an emergency situation, your moral, ethical conclusion will also be different in a particular situation.

Check your understanding of Lesson 1

1. When and how did Western philosophy start?
2. What is the central question that ethics is dealing with?
3. What is the working definition of ethics?
4. What are the three main ethical theories?

2.2 Lesson 2: Moral dilemmas

Objectives

On completing this lesson, the reader will understand:

- The five criteria of a moral dilemma
- How to use the five criteria to identify a dilemma as a moral dilemma
- How to distinguish a moral dilemma as 'personalistic'
- What professional codes are and when to use them
- The three reasons for a compromise
- The procedure to achieve moral quality
- The 'step-by-step' scheme to describe, analyse and solve a moral dilemma and how to use the scheme.

It is not always clear when ethics are at stake. People, groups of people, feelings, motives and intentions, and elements of personality can be morally right or wrong. In this book we focus on the actions of human beings.

All kinds of object are good or not good in a non-moral sense: for example, physical objects such as cars and paintings. A car can be a good means of transport. That doesn't have anything—certainly at first sight—to do with ethics.

The question of whether ethics are at stake can be answered in several ways.

Some colleagues at the Christian University for Applied Economic Studies choose a simple solution. They argue that a matter is presented as a moral, ethical dilemma when there are moral, ethical assumptions involved (Meykamp, Westerhuis and Terpstra 1989: 28-34).

A matter can also be non-moral. In that case you can choose to add the moral, ethical perspective. We can ask when and why the actions in that particular case are morally right or wrong, good or not good.

Beauchamp (2001: 15) suggests a pluralistic solution. A judgement, principle or ideal is no longer moral on the basis of one criterion, but on the basis of several criteria. This opinion leads to the scheme.

M1	M2	M3	M4	M5
ABCD	ABCE	ABDE	ACDE	BCDE

M1 to M5 are moral statements. The criteria are:

A = great social interest

B = tries to minimise opposing interests in society

C = is deduced from philosophical views of life that are meant to guide human actions

D = generalises and prescribes human actions

E = has authority and is able to override non-moral rules

Moral dilemmas differ from other dilemmas. They have to meet **five criteria**:

1. You can't avoid the dilemma. You are at a fork in the road; you have to go left or right. Even when you don't make a choice, you are choosing

2. Other people are involved, even when they are far away

3. Any choice you make is of interest to those involved. It can have consequences for the feelings of self-respect or happiness of other people

Environmental ethics challenges (2) and (3). If you consider that people who are involved have an interest, should you also consider the involvement of other living beings, elements of nature or even nature as a whole?

1. You can't satisfy all the interests 100%; you can't completely satisfy everyone

2. The moral actor is free to choose

In professional ethics it is also important to make sure that the moral dilemma is within your personal sphere of control. If you try to identify, analyse and solve professional moral dilemmas yourself, they should not be of a structural character. If they are, you should consult a union, a political party or some other organisation that can take care of big problems. So if there are problems concerning environment, health and safety that can be solved only by building a new plant, you have to consider whether that is within your span of control. Many professional groups use a professional ethical code when they have to deal with moral, ethical dilemmas. See, for instance, the US National Society of Professional Engineers, in particular the Ethic Case Search,[5] and the British Society of Environmental Engineers Code of Conduct.[6]

To give an idea of a continuum on this issue, we can use the example of hunger: year after year we are confronted with hunger in different parts of the world. We can help by donating money and sending bread and fish. Some people say that is no solution to the problem. People in need of food have to learn how to plant seed and how to fish. They can be helped with machinery to plough the land and manage the water and by fishing boats. Others say hunger is a fault in the capitalist system. When you want to take hunger out of the world, you have to start by dealing with capitalism. These solutions range from personalistic to structural.

According to a psychologist Lawrence Kohlberg, there are three stages in moral development: pre-conventional (solely concerned with self), conventional (judging the morality of actions by comparing

5 www.nspe.org/Ethics/EthicsResources/index.html, accessed 20 March 2012.
6 environmental.org.uk/index.php?page=code-of-coduct, accessed 20 March 2012.

them to society's expectations) and post-conventional (realisation that the individual's own perspective may take precedence over society's view). Moral ethical maturity equals the post-conventional stage, when you don't need a code or guide (which might 'pin you down' at the conventional stage) because you know what your own values and principles are and you act according to them.

Before going on to look at step-by-step schemes for dealing with moral dilemmas, we will briefly discuss how to achieve moral quality when we are confronted with a moral dilemma in a professional situation. How do we make sure that the professional action we take has moral quality?

The first point is about the action itself and the second about the procedure.

According to Van Hilhorst (1989: 112-15, 117) the **action** has moral quality when it is a compromise. There are three reasons:

1. Professional action takes part within a community. In a community people have several different interests. When, for example, persons A, B and C formulate their interests according to Figure 2.3a they can't come to an agreement. So they have to choose a start as shown in Figure 2.3b. In Figure 2.3b it is possible to make a decision that meets, at least in part, all three interests (X)

2. In most situations a compromise is better than a choice based on a principle. Acting according to a principle or a rule can damage the actor, the company or society as a whole

3. The third reason for compromise is that in a professional situation you often have to make a choice from only 'bad' possibilities. Daily reality is rarely paradise and you are not the one who can change that. So you have to settle for achieving as much as you can

So the first thing to do when you are confronted with a moral dilemma is to make calculations of good versus bad, benefit versus harm, advantage versus disadvantage. This is utilitarian ethics. There are situations that involve basic rules, norms and values, like justice or the right to life. You know immediately what you ought to do, so you don't have to calculate.

Figure 2.3a **Inability to reach agreement**

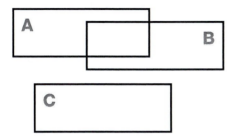

Figure 2.3b **Common areas of agreement**

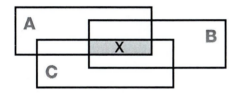

Moral quality can only be reached when you follow a procedure that is characterised by the word 'together'. Together with the people that are involved, you recognise that the problem is a moral one; together you analyse and talk things over; and together you decide what to do.

Meykamp, Westerhuis and Terpstra (1989) have developed a step-by-step scheme to describe, analyse, assess and justify a moral dilemma.

2.2.1 Step-by-step scheme for the assessment of a moral problem

Step 1: Description and analysis

- Briefly describe the situation

- Who is involved in the situation?

- What are the different interests of the people involved? Which interest can be influenced in favour and which against?

- What solution can be reached by one person if he or she doesn't need to take account of the other people involved?

Step 2: Assessment

- Whose interests have to weigh most? Formulate those interests by using utilitarian argumentation (benefit, happiness)
- Whose interests are harmed by that choice? Formulate those interests by using utilitarian argumentation (harm, pain)
- Make a proposal on how to compensate for that harm
- Are there any basic principles at stake in the situation? If so formulate those interests by using deontological argumentation
- To what extent do those basic principles have to be taken into account in the search for a solution?
- Describe the final solution

Step 3: Justification

- Which utilitarian arguments have determined the final choice?
- Did deontological arguments play a role?
- Was the choice made on the basis of 'walking in someone else's shoes' (imagining oneself in the other's place)?
- What view of humans and society forms the basis of the choice?

It is important to note that the step-by-step scheme is a tool to help to solve moral dilemmas. It isn't a cure-all.

Check your understanding of Lesson 2

1. What are the five criteria of a moral dilemma?
2. Give an example of a moral dilemma using the five criteria
3. Is the dilemma a 'personalistic' one?
4. What is a professional code and how can you use it?
5. What are the three reasons for a compromise?
6. What is the procedure to achieve moral quality?
7. What is the step-by-step scheme to describe, analyse, assess and justify a moral dilemma?
8. What is the outcome when you use the scheme for the moral dilemma you described earlier?

2.3 Lesson 3: Defining environmental ethics

Environmental ethics is about moral care for nature and environment. That moral care depends on what is and what has the moral status. You can give moral status to nature and environment based on both anthropocentric and non-anthropocentric arguments. The most important theories of both arguments are dealt with in this chapter.

Objectives

On completing this lesson, the reader will be able to:
- Give a definition of environmental ethics
- Give a definition of environment
- Give examples of environmental problems that raise ethical questions
- Understand the two main approaches of environmental ethics: the anthropocentric and the non-anthropocentric
- Understand the characteristics of four theories within the anthropocentric view

Case study 2.1 **Experiments on animals**

What attitude should human beings take towards nature and environment? How should you act towards animals, plants, water, soil, air, species and ecosystems? What questions arise when you are confronted with a video on experiments on animals? The video is made in cooperation with institutions that carry out those experiments. It offers you balanced information on the topic. The central question is: how far do you go in using animals for experiments? Maybe better: how far are you allowed to go? The question arises when you consider how much we love animals, especially when they are our pets.

- You hear and see a pet bird in a cage that sings and is cared for. How far do you go in keeping pet birds?
- You are confronted with a monkey doing an act or with chickens on a grill. We love animals. How far do you go in using animals for entertainment or eating them?
- When animals are used to conduct medical experiments for the benefit of other animals and humans, the question is also: how far do you go?

Some experts say that experiments on animals haven't contributed at all to today's medical knowledge and practice. Others say that very important medical developments such as the control and cure of fatal diseases are due to animal experimentation. Both kinds of experts ask you again: how far do you go?

Case study 2.2 **The essen landscape**

In the Netherlands, especially in the east, you can find a landscape called *essen*. *Essen* (the singular *es* means open field) are farmlands around villages, taking a spherical form.

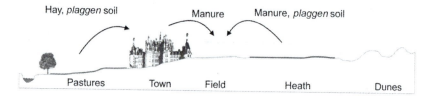

Around the year 1000, vigorous population growth in the Netherlands meant that more farmland was needed to produce food. The farmland had to be fertilised. This was done in several ways, but mostly with dung from sheep. During the day the sheep grazed on the heath. At night they came back to the villages, producing dung there. In the wintertime the sheep were fed with the hay from the meadows. Because the sheep were grazing (and defecating) on the heath, the farmers also used sods of turf from the heath, known as *plaggen*, to fertilise the farmland. This movement of *plaggen* and dung gradually built up.

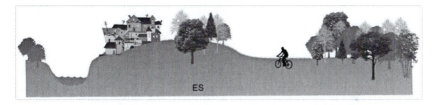

So the *es* is born. It is a mound formed on the landscape, some ten hectares wide. The mound is striking because it has an open and wide view. It is traditionally used only for agriculture, so there are no hedges or woods. Some have a solitary oak as a marker in the landscape, from which several roads run in all directions. At the edge of the mound you can find woods. Farms and villages are close by. *Essen* are prized for their natural, cultural and historical values.

Because of industrialisation and population growth there is a plan to build some factories and four apartments on an *es*. How far do you go in changing the landscape?

2.3.1 Definitions

A definition of environmental ethics

In Lesson 1 we found a working definition for ethics.

According to that definition we can present one for environmental ethics:

> Systematic thinking
> about the action
> of humans
> towards nature and environment,
> asking the question
> whether that action is good/not good
> in the end.

The definition of environmental ethics raises three questions. First, what human actions lead to ethical reflection? Second, what is the definition of nature and environment? Third, we have to decide what environmental ethics means with regard to 'good in the end'. The first two questions are dealt with when we provide a definition of nature and the environment and when we consider environmental problems. To give an answer to the third question, we look at environmental problems as conflicts of values and which end-value will guide actions. There are two perspectives from which to analyse those conflicts: the anthropocentric and the non-anthropocentric. Both perspectives lead to several ethical theories.

The definition of nature and environment

The word 'environment' originates from ecology. Ecology studies the relation between organisms and their surroundings, mostly the natural surroundings that have influence on the organisms. The environmental sciences present two limitations.

On the one hand, the environment is the physical surroundings of a human. Physical means the living (biotic) and the non-living (abiotic) surroundings. On the other hand, because humans are seen as social beings we talk about the relationship between society and environment. One definition of environment is:

The physical non-living and living surroundings of society. Society and those surroundings have a reciprocal relationship.

Although the environment can be seen and studied at different levels,[7] nature and the environment, which are mentioned in the definition of environmental ethics, have to be considered in a broad sense. When we talk about human actions towards nature and environment, we mean towards:

- Animals
- Plants and other (micro-)organisms
- Water, air and soil
- Seas, rivers and landscapes
- Ecosystems

You can even conclude that human actions towards nature and the environment mostly concern actions towards nature and elements of nature.

In Figure 2.4 humans and nature and environment are shown as separate. The elements of nature and environment are concentric circles, each circle with a new entity or element. Environmental ethics asks which if any of these have moral relevance and status.

---

7   According to Van Ast and Geerlings (1993), the environment can be studied at different levels. The levels can be seen as:
  1. Factors or components
  2. Compartments
  3. Systems
The levels are shown in four figures in the Appendix to Chapter 2.

Figure 2.4 **Schematic presentation of humans and nature and environment**

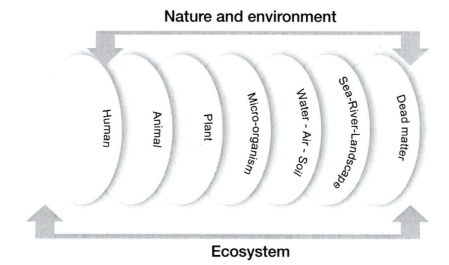

2.3.2 Environmental problems

Environmental science studies the relation between humans and the environment. On the one hand, the environment has a meaning for human beings. They are dependent on the environment for their existence. On the other hand, human activities influence the environment. The relation between humans and environment is reciprocal (see Fig. 2.5).

Figure 2.5 **The relation between humans and the environment**

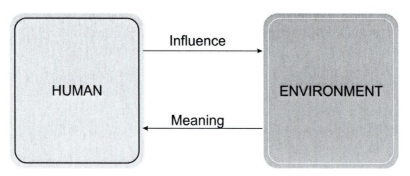

The environment has **meaning** for humans in three ways:

- It is a condition of life

- It has intrinsic value

- It is a means of production

In the first meaning the dependence on the environment is strongest. Human beings need a good environment for their health and for food. A good environment can also have a psychological effect on human beings. The second, intrinsic, value has to do with the ethical question of whether nature and environment—and elements of them—have a value separate from the instrumental value we give them. Third, humans use natural resources, air, water and soil as their means of production.

All human actions have an effect or an **influence** on nature and the environment. Humans can add something to or remove something from the environment. Humans can also change the shape or the structure of the environment, for example, by urbanisation, exploitation or blocking the mouth of a river. These actions don't necessarily cause an environmental problem.

There is an environmental problem when humans themselves consider that the relationship with the environment is disturbed. This happens when one of the three meanings loses so much quality that a group of people considers it problematic. So environmental problems are not those of the individual but social problems.

Based on the three types of human influence (adding, removing or changing structure), three types of disturbance to the environment, that is, effects that cause problems, can be distinguished (see Fig. 2.6). Disturbance by means of addition is called pollution. Disturbance by removal is called exhaustion. Other disturbances—changes in the structure of the environment—are referred to as violation.

Figure 2.6 **Disturbance of the environment**

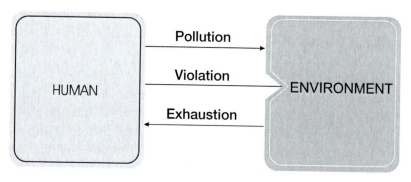

Moreover, environmental problems can be seen as conflicts of value. A situation becomes an environmental problem when we realise that there is a difference between the actual and the desired situation of nature and environment.

Both the actual situation and the desired one are loaded with values. According to a Dutch philosopher, Wouter Achterberg (1994), environmental problems can be seen as conflicts of value. That leads to two questions: what are the values and how can conflicts of value be solved? According to Achterberg, in general conflicts are between material or social values on one side and environmental values on the other. Examples are:

- Survival, prosperity, health and employment
- Distributive justice and freedom
- Safe and clean environment, sustainability and a rich and varied nature

The solution of conflicts of value brings you to the question of which action is good in the end. You already know this question from the working definition of environmental ethics. Environmental ethics help you to analyse and to solve conflicts of value. Moreover, it has to justify the solutions. This involves answering questions such as who or what has value and what kind of values are we talking about?

There are two large groups of value perspectives: the anthropocentric and the non-anthropocentric. Both cover different environmental ethics. The distinction between anthropocentrism and non-anthropo-centrism is whether only human beings have value or whether other elements of nature and environment also have value. Who or what has moral status and why?

2.3.3 Moral care of nature

Environmental ethics emerged as a new sub-discipline of philoso-phy in the early 1970s. Until then philosophy had been questioning human actions towards human beings. Actions towards nature were dealt with in an anthropocentric way. Actions were good or not good according to the well-being of humans.

Since the 1970s, traditional anthropocentrism has been challenged. In the first place, environmental ethics questions the assumed moral superiority of human beings over members of other species on earth. In the second place, it investigates the possibility of rational argu-ments for assigning intrinsic value to the natural environment and its non-human contents.

There are two main approaches to environmental ethics:

- The anthropocentric approach

- The non-anthropocentric approach

These two approaches or views of moral care for nature will be treated extensively in Chapter 4. Meanwhile we offer a short intro-duction here.

The anthropocentric approach

The debate on the possible intrinsic value and the ethical consid-eration of nature is part of a larger debate on the status of so-called 'anthropocentrism', or human-centred ethical thinking. Anthro-pocentrics deny the physiocentrists' claim that there is an intrinsic value of natural beings or nature as a whole. In other words, within the field of environmental ethics the anthropocentric and physi-ocentric positions are sharply opposed. In the anthropocentric view, animals, plants, ecosystems and the whole of nature have only an instrumental value for human beings and their interests. The only value in nature lies in the satisfaction of basic human needs: for example, human nourishment depends on nature. The only reason to hold back in using natural resources (animals, fossil fuels, etc.) is out of consideration for the needs of contemporary humans or, at most, future generations. However, some more moderate anthropocentrics may concede that an aesthetic argument for protecting nature can be add to this instrumental view: nature's sensual attractions for us, such as the pleasure we take in breathing fresh mountain air. For now, the question persists: Which has priority? The welfare of humans or the welfare of animals and plants involved, possibly in an 'intact' nature?

The non-anthropocentric approach

By contrast, there are many ethicists who try to widen the 'moral community' to include non-humans. The non-anthropocentric view can be presented in many ways. In this book the view is presented as four theories:

1. Pathocentrism

2. Biocentrism

3. Ecocentrism

4. Holism

Each theory deals with the question of which elements of nature and environment are candidates for moral status and what is the argument for moral status. The argumentation often can be seen as a part of the main ethical theories we saw in Lesson 1. Here we give a short introduction. The four theories and their representatives will be dealt with in Chapter 4.

The essence of the four can be found by looking at the meaning of the Greek roots.

1. **Pathocentrism** is derived from the Greek *pathos*, meaning 'feeling'. Pathocentrism gives moral status to all beings that can have pleasure and pain, can suffer and are 'sentient' and says that making sentient beings suffer is wrong

2. **Biocentrism** is derived from *bios*, meaning 'life'. Biocentrism gives moral status to all living beings

3. **Ecocentrism** is from *eco*, meaning 'house', and is mostly used to mean environment. In ecology it is the surroundings a being is living in. Mostly there is interdependence between the being(s) and the surrounding, nature and environment. That interdependence is also the characteristic of an eco-system. So the moral status of an ecosystem and its members is at stake in ecocentrism. Ecocentrism deals with the moral status of larger entities such as species and ecosystems

4. The difference between ecocentrism and **holism** (Greek *holos*, meaning 'whole' or 'all') is not always clear, but holism has to do with the moral status of the 'whole'. That can mean 'Gaia', 'Mother Earth' or nature. The elements of the whole, of the ecosystem, are depending on the well-being of that whole. That is the argument to give moral status to the whole and its elements. Holism puts also forward the question of the moral status of rocks, rivers, landscape, etc.

Check your understanding of Lesson 3

1. What is the working definition of environmental ethics?
2. What is the definition of nature and the environment?
3. What are environmental problems?
4. Which environmental problems provoke ethical questions?
5. What are the two main approaches within environmental ethics?
6. What are the characteristics of four theories within the second main approach?

Appendix to Chapter 2

Figure 2.7a **The environment in compartments**

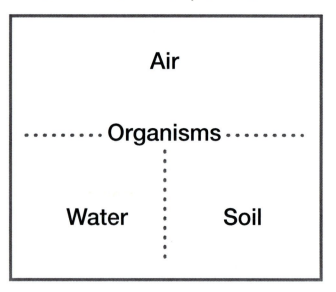

Figure 2.7b **System levels**

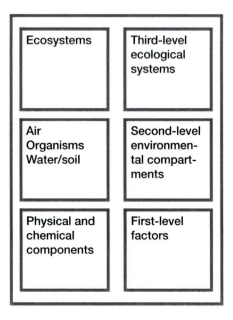

Figure 2.7c **The environment**

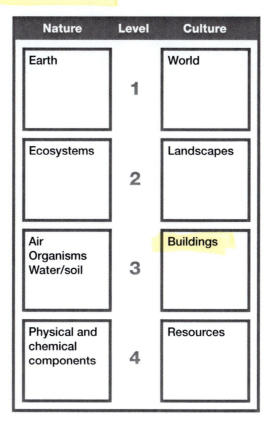

Nature	Level	Culture
Earth	1	World
Ecosystems	2	Landscapes
Air Organisms Water/soil	3	Buildings
Physical and chemical components	4	Resources

Figure 2.7d **The environment considered at three system levels**
Source: Van Ast and Geerlings 1993

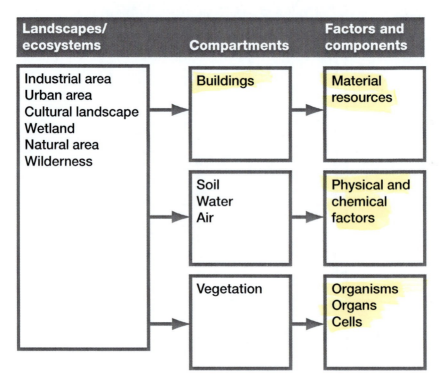

3

The challenge to environmental ethics

Rainer Paslack

Central goals

The reader should understand how the field of environmental ethics is structured, the central areas of environmental ethics (Lesson 1), and the essential levels of environmental reasoning (Lesson 2).

3.1 Lesson 1: Three areas of environmental ethics

Objectives

On completing this lesson, the reader will be able to:

- Describe the central fields and questions of environmental ethics
- Explain what is meant by 'a non-human being can possess a value in itself'
- Discuss the differences between a direct or indirect ethical obligation to nature

Ethical reflection is an essential part of practical philosophy. It tries to give answers to the question 'What should we do?' Ethics aims to provide a normative orientation for human action. The relation between the actors is of particular importance: in accordance with which underlying criteria shall the interaction between people take place? Further: how is a given situation to be assessed, in order to behave in an ethically correct manner? Universal ethics (as, e.g., Immanuel Kant defines it) proceeds on the assumption that all moral subjects are axiomatically co-equal and therefore are to be treated according to the same criteria. Social distinctions are therefore basically irrelevant: from the standpoint of ethics, which lays universal claim to validation, all human (rational) subjects are of the same value. Therefore, the acts of all humans are to be subject to the same criteria and 'moral imperatives'. Thus, for example, lying is forbidden without exception for all human subjects. 'White' lies might be acceptable under certain circumstances, but sanction can never be given to untruthfulness in principal. What applies to one person applies to any other person as well. Whoever wants to be acknowledged by another person as a moral being, and wants to be treated in a just way, has to be willing on his or her part to accept the morality and dignity of any other person and treat him or her with justice (principle of equality and principle of reciprocity). Without these principles there would be no general human rights, and democratic societies would not be legitimised.

In general, ethics examines what is valuable in individual and social life, in relation to the world, in so far as ethical behaviour always consists of implementing ethical values. At the outset it may not be evident exactly which values are valid for all people (or ethical beings) and how in detail justice can prevail among people (what exactly is meant by 'distributive justice' or 'justice of performance'?). Nevertheless there are certain ethical principles the globalised world cannot forgo, if it wants to live in peace: for this the Universal Declaration of Human Rights[1] provides the foundation. Certain ethical values in mind-set and behaviour are necessary in order to lay down binding rules for a harmonious social, political, economic and cultural intercourse of people and nations and to be able to maintain

---

1 See www. un. org/en/documents/udhr, accessed 25 March 2012.

it permanently. Yet how certain core values such as freedom, equality and solidarity are to be interpreted needs to be negotiated frequently on an interpersonal, intercultural and international level. In interpreting even such high-ranking values as human rights, conflicts of interest and values arise, as happens when the world-view of different people is affected by different religious, ethnic and political viewpoints that are not compatible. And there may be different reasons lying behind the same values when people come from different philosophical and ideological backgrounds. This can lead to different priorities of the values (within the hierarchy of values) and consequences for behaviour; so, for example, the value 'solidarity' is presented differently from a utilitarian position than from a Kantian or a Christian viewpoint.

A special problem in applying values originates when it is not really clear what belongs to the 'ethical universe'. Environmental ethics has this application problem. Environmental ethics is an ethics of application. Its worth depends on whether moral intrinsic value is attached to the environment of the human society—that is, nature—or not. It is indisputable that nature is valuable for humans; but does nature own, as a whole, a value in itself, or do certain natural entities hold a value in themselves, as is considered to be the case for people? In other words, does nature—or do natural beings—own an intrinsic (absolute) value or only a relative (derived) value in relation to the good of humans (individuals or society as a whole)? Many environmental ethicists are of the opinion that such an autonomous value needs to be conferred on certain beings in the natural environment of humans, which has to be respected in our relations with them. Later we will amplify

> **Moral concern and self-interest**
>
> To have moral concern or respect for others means to place intrinsic value on their good life, to further their happiness for its own sake and not solely for the sake of your own happiness. A self-interested agent, in contrast, accords the happiness of others only instrumental value for his or her own happiness. That moral concern has something to do with an unselfish regard for the good life of all others is accepted by virtually all contemporary moral theories (Krebs 1999: 16).

the different reasons for such an extension of the 'moral community' to nature.

Even though if one confines oneself to ascribing an *indirect* value to nature that only exists in relation to humans and their needs and interests, environmental ethics poses a challenge to the ethical, political and economic behaviour of people towards their natural environment. It constitutes a field with new forms of evaluation: for example, how one should proceed with scarce natural resources (e.g. fossil fuels), of which unconsidered waste can lead to a crisis for future generations. The interest in an immediate use comes into conflict with the interest in provisions for the future. We will return to that.

We can distinguish three areas of environmental ethics, which together build an ascending sequence. Each subsequent area includes the former or extends it with an additional 'moral agent'.

Check your understanding of Lesson 1

1. Why are principles such as the principle of equality and the principle of reciprocity essential for any ethics that puts the focus on the dignity of humankind and a just society?
2. Why are conflicts of interests and values unavoidable in our modern society?
3. What is the basic question to which environmental ethics tries to give an answer?
4. What is the difference between a *direct* and an *indirect* ethical obligation to nature?

3.1.1 Ethics of resources

When a value is given to nature only in relation to humans, we talk about ethics of resources. Of course, the ethics of resources is environmental ethics only in a narrower sense; nevertheless, it always remains a part of every broader definition of environmental ethics. The ethics of resources places humans in the centre of its interests by scrutinising aspects of the handling of scarce, exhaustible raw materials and environmental media such as water, soil and air. Special ethical considerations are focused on renewable biotic resources such as forests and fishing resources. Questions about a dangerous change in the earth's climate also belong to the field of resource ethics. Not least, agricultural ethics belongs to this form of environmental ethics and particularly engages in questions of changes to soil and landscape. Grave environmental damage is caused especially by the agricultural utilisation of the environment.

Resource ethics asks how we can use the raw materials and environmental media (such as water and soil) provided by nature without causing irreversible damage (over-exploitation or environmental pollution). Such ethics can be justified solely for anthropocentric reasons: that is, by the interests of people.

3.1.2 Animal ethics

Animal ethics is concerned with the well-being of individual beings that are sensitive to pain. The term 'animal ethics' is a bit ambiguous, as animal ethics usually only applies to *sentient* organisms. Thereby the animal kingdom is divided into animals with a nerve system and animals that lack sensitivity (to pain) because of the absence of a nerve system. The leading assumption here is that the existence of a nerve system is a prerequisite for a capacity to suffer. In any case, animal ethics views the relationship of humans to all such natural beings by assuming they are able to suffer in the same way as we do. We can empathise with a sentient being, because the animal as a 'suffering creature' is sibling-like, associated with humans. Furthermore, such beings possess a distinct instinct for self-preservation—in the way they pursue interests, search for satisfaction and strive to avoid suffering and dislike.

Organisms that have an interest in themselves, however, notably appear as morally valuable, because one has to acknowledge a certain autonomy in their behaviour. This is not only valid for the big apes, which are our nearest relatives in the animal kingdom, but also for all non-primates, presuming that they have sensitivity to pain and obviously have a self-conscious perception of their environment.

So animal ethics asks whether animals—at least the ones with sensitivity to pain—possess a value and a purpose in themselves, and—if so—asks what this means in an ethical sense with regard to our relationship and behaviour towards them. Consequently, animal ethics moves beyond the sole anthropocentric approach by thinking in a 'pathocentric' way.

3.1.3 Ethics of nature

The ethics of nature attends to the moral aspects of dealing with lower 'insentient' life forms (plants, fungi, bacteria, etc.) as well as with other supra-individual biotic entities as species, ecosystems and landscapes. In the form of 'conservation ethics' it discusses questions of preservation of natural areas to protect them from destruction by humans. In this sense it will contribute to the environment-related protection of civilisation. In a narrower sense the ethics of nature deals with the determination of the moral status of nature or larger natural systems (ecosystems). We will see later that the substantiation of nature ethics will confront us with most difficult problems. The main concern is not with individual ethics referring to single organisms and the protection of certain individual beings, but about supra-individual entities: for example, species conservation, perhaps even the protection of evolutionary potentials or processes. In this case nature ethics is 'biocentrically' (all living beings) or 'ecocentrically' (ecological systems) or even 'holistically' (all natural things) oriented. Nature's ethical considerations touch on difficult natural philosophical questions. For example: Does nature as a whole hold a moral status? Do the protective rights of biotopes (habitats of organisms) rank higher than the protective rights of single organisms and species, so that we have to sacrifice single organisms or even whole populations in favour of the conservation of larger ecosystems? Nature ethics asks whether each form of life or complex natural systems—and perhaps even nature as a whole—possesses moral value and therefore is absolutely worthy of protection. Such ethics (however it might be substantiated) goes—even more than the animal ethics—beyond the scope of an environmental ethics that respects the interests solely of humans. Instead of anthropocentric,

> Only when the last tree has died and the last river has been poisoned and the last fish has been caught will we realise that we cannot eat money (A prophecy of a nineteenth-century Cree Indian made popular by Greenpeace).

nature ethics is physiocentric oriented (see Eser and Potthast 1999; Krebs 1999).

To finish this section let us look briefly at the historic development of these three areas of the environmental ethics.

Historically, **resource ethics** is the oldest form of environmental ethics. In earlier times, people were already wondering how existing natural materials, such as the wood of the forests or water, could be used in a sustainable (protecting) manner. This was based on experience of the desolation of entire regions that had been cleared completely for construction and shipbuilding (the ancient Greeks, who maintained large fleets, had already noticed this with pain); or on experience of the contamination of waters that had been used too intensively for tanning skins and dyeing textiles. The resource-ethics debate reached a first culminating point in the 1970s with the realisation of the 'limits to growth', as the Club of Rome[2] warned of the overexploitation of fossil fuels and natural metal deposits.

Animal ethics also has old philosophical roots, with Immanuel Kant postulating a prescription of brute contact with sentient animals (in contrast with René Descartes who, still thinking mechanistically, had viewed animals as dumb machines). Furthermore, as Kant believed, considerate contact with animals could contribute to the moral improvement of the humans. Even the utilitarian Jeremy Bentham formulated a primary obligation of humans towards sentient animals.

Nature ethics, in the form of conservation ethics, refers back to the age of Romanticism (end of the 18th century until the mid-19th century), as the beauty of landscapes was appreciated extensively for the first time (see Pfordten 1996; Thomas 1983). The contribution of the aesthetic feeling for nature to the emergence of environmental ethics cannot be estimated highly enough. This is still valid today. In the tradition of the romantic philosophy of nature the home and nature conservation movement began in Europe and North America in the 19th century: here for the first time, criticism of civilisation and technology was joined with national homeland 'connectedness' and the feeling of a deep bond with nature. This connection is still alive in

2 See www.clubofrome.org/eng/home, accessed 25 March 2012.

miscellaneous varieties of eco-philosophy or 'deep ecology' as well as in the green movement.[3]

Environmental ethics as an autonomous academic field, however, began only around 1970, as the threat to the natural livelihood of humans from pollution and ecological destruction became obvious. It was only then that the scientific exploration of complex natural systems (ecology and ecosystem research) and interactions between ecosystems and economies had progressed far enough so that arguments from environmental ethics could now also be backed up scientifically. Resource ethics especially, but also landscape ethics, experienced an immense upswing in the context of 'ecological ethics'.

This development was accompanied by a strong change of public awareness towards

---

To the argument of aesthetic contemplation

Mr K and Nature
Asked about his attitude to nature, Mr. K said: 'Now and then I like to see a few trees on coming out of the house particularly because they achieve such a special degree of reality by looking so different according to the time of day and season. Also, as time goes on, we city dwellers get dazed by never seeing anything but use-objects, such as houses and railways which, if unoccupied, would be empty, if unused, meaningless. Our peculiar social system allows us to regard even human beings as such use-objects; and so trees, at any rate for me, since I am not a carpenter, have something soothingly independent about them, outside myself, and as a matter of fact I hope that for carpenters, too, they have something about them which cannot be put to use' (Brecht 1961: 110).

---

a distinct environmental consciousness. For the first time the green movement was able to articulate its protest against the destruction and the blight of the natural environment by founding green parties. Many of them were elected into their national parliaments and so could work politically.

---

3 The phrase 'deep ecology' was introduced in 1972 by the philosopher and mountaineer Arne Naess to mean a holistic relationship between humans and nature.

At that time it became very obvious to many people around the globe, that the reflection on the relationship between humans, society and nature should be an integral part of *all* ethics. Animal protectionists could now exert their concern for better protection of sentient animals more effectively: this pertained to the treatment of animals in agriculture (animal husbandry) and in research (animal experiments), but also included an understanding that the continuing (danger of) extinction of species (birds, whales, big apes, etc.) needed to be stopped. The demand for the ethically appropriate treatment of animals and for the protection of endangered species, as well as significant ecosystems (e.g. tropical rainforests) that contribute to the world climate as well as providing a habitat, became unmistakable.

It is clear that a conflict within environmental ethics between an anthropocentric and a physiocentric ethics was bound to happen. How are the particular interests of humans and animals (plants, biotopes, species, etc.) to be ethically weighed against each other? In which cases do the interests of humans have to take second place to the interests of other living beings? Environmental ethicists have not only to assert their demands against economic and social interests but also to crusade in internal conflicts for the 'right' environmental ethics.

Check your understanding of Lesson 2

1. What are the natural resources in question in the ethics of resources?
2. Does animal ethics refer to *all* animals?
3. How can one determine whether a living being possesses an interest in itself or self-awareness?
4. Does the ethics of nature also include *inanimate* objects? For example: minerals or comets?
5. In what sense may climate have an ethical value so that it should be preserved?
6. Could a conflict occur between the attempt to preserve whole ecosystems and the intention to protect single living beings?
7. In what sense are humans part of nature and in what sense are they opposed to nature?

3.2 **Lesson 2: Three levels of environmental reasoning**

Objectives

On completing this lesson, the reader will be able to:

- Recognise the levels of environmental thinking that environmental ethics can contribute to
- Describe how environmental ethics can influence eco-political decisions
- Explain what natural sciences and environmental ethics can learn from one another
- Point out how difficult it is to determine the success of environmental measures
- Outline why humans should be interested in the protection of nature

Earlier we distinguished three fields of environmental ethics: resource ethics, animal ethics and nature ethics. This division can be abolished in certain cases. Discrimination is applied analytically but not categorically. Some environmental problems—such as the protection of water in the foundation of natural parks, in spacious urban planning, etc.—have aspects of all three: resource, animal and nature ethics.

In order to establish a classification of environmental ethics it is important not only to discriminate between the three fields (among environmental ethicists these are largely agreed), but also to distinguish the different levels on which environmental ethics are implemented. According to Konrad Ott (2000), three such levels can be outlined:

1. Philosophical level (ethics)

2. Political–legal level (laws)

3. Casuistic level (single cases and actions)

Each level requires a different sphere of activity but these levels are built on each other: public measures in reference to single cases (environmental management) have to be legally protected. The law for its part has to be based on ethical principles.

3.2.1 Philosophical level

This 'high' level deals with fundamental explanatory statements: ethical claims of validity are raised that should be applied universally: that is, for all members of the ethical discourse community. In the philosophical universe of discourse on environmental ethics the pros and cons of certain positions are developed and discussed. The participants of this discussion are the academic ethics experts (environmental ethicists) and all people who have to make environmental decisions in their vocational context (politicians and jurists, but also engineers, biotechnologists, etc.). In an extended framework all people can participate in the environmental debate if they possess a developed environmental consciousness (as well as a certain scientific education) and when they wish to account for their actions towards the environment. Among the participants of the environmental discourse all non-philosophers, of course, are dependent on preparatory work from the environmental experts for a better understanding and orientation: they expect well-founded proposals for environmentally compatible behaviour and an argued solution to environmental ethical conflicts.

However, *within* environmental ethics—as mentioned above— there are controversies among environmental ethicists that make orientation difficult; in particular, the anthropocentric and physiocentric positions are opposed sharply. For the broader public it is not possible offhand to comprehend the pros and cons of arguments concerning the alternatives presented by philosophers. However, when the internal philosophical debate does not lead to any objectively valid results, environment-ethical counselling of the public and especially the decision-makers (politicians, engineers, etc.) is possible only in a limited way. Ultimately each person and each society has to decide for itself to what extent it wants to give importance—besides the anthropocentric arguments—to physiocentric arguments

If and how far animal and nature ethical aspects will play a role in the behaviour of people and societies has to be decided by each person *individually* or—on the national and international level—politically. In order that these decisions are not ill founded or made merely intuitively, it is necessary to gain a profound understanding of the controversial discussions within professional environmental ethics.

3.2.2 Political–legal level

On this level we are dealing with the definition of collective, binding, normative regulations and aims for political actions (e.g. environmental-quality goals). Every definition of this kind presupposes certain environmental attitudes and other political decisions in the past. All relevant environmental aims and programmes are decided and set in force by political organs such as governments, parliaments and public administrations. The most important instrument in this process is the existing environmental law. **Environmental law** combines ethical principles and the results of political decision-making in the form of laws and other ordinances that are obligatory for all citizens of a state. The coverage of legal directives is normally extensive (we will examine this more closely in Chapter 5): not only strict binding laws but also guidelines, quotas and standards may be defined. Within the context of political–legal regulation, environmental consulting can help to weigh different individual and collective claims and rights to use environmental resources and media (such as water, soil or air). To what extent has an industrial entrepreneur the right to free use without contamination of water or soil? How far can liberal societies restrain individual rights in favour of communal rights? Under what conditions can the claim of protecting the workplace and the societal claim of conserving an intact and healthy environment live in harmony? More generally, how can we harmonise a consistent environment policy with legitimate economic interests? How is it possible to achieve long-term environmental political aims of sustainability (e.g. concerning the consumption of fossil fuels or other raw materials) and short-term interests of private profit?

Environmental ethics can contribute to making environment policies efficient and to raising public awareness and consciousness. For example, the environmental ethicist may leave inner academic circles and intervene in the public debate about the definition of climate goals, the rescue of tropical rainforests or fish stocks in the oceans, or about the problem of 'environmental justice' (the disadvantage or discrimination of marginal groups in their own society or of people in the developing world). In particular, the skills of environmental ethicists are required to determine environmental aims, quality standards and limits of reasonability, because in these cases the qualitative dimension of environmental political and legal decisions is affected. An adequate determination of the relationship between people and society on the one hand and nature on the other is an essential precondition for regulating behaviour towards the natural environment, because environmental ethics provides the arguments to legitimise our behaviour as acceptable.

3.2.3 Casuistic level

At the centre of the casuistic level are tangible cases of environmental contamination or destruction, responsible methods and measures for the protection or regeneration of a polluted or destroyed environment. Primarily, these measures are of a technical kind. Practical environmental management is required, and the know-how of environmental experts (environmental engineers, technicians, etc.) is central. Although environmental ethics cannot directly contribute to the technical solutions of environmental problems, it can enquire into the sense and significance of technological measures and of their normative legitimisation. And environmental ethics can assess alternative technical solutions, where the depth of intervention, the costs and the possible unintended side-effects of the submitted solutions are different. The execution of technical measures does not take place in an ethics-free room: such actions always touch collective or individual interests or rights protected by law as well as having to take account of the different interests and claims of people involved. Who has the disadvantage? Who bears the costs? How sustainable should the effects of the intended measure be? In an ethical comparison of alternative technological conceptions or programmes, especially, conflicts can arise between anthropocentric and physiocentric perspectives. What is most worthy of protection in such a case? Which has priority: the welfare of humans or the welfare of animals and plants involved in the environmental problem?

Furthermore, is the intended measure even appropriate, if the given environmental problem is very complex and the success of the intended measure is uncertain? Technical interventions into complex ecosystems always take place with a certain uncertainty: will the desired effects be reached or not? And will unintended (and unexpected) effects outweigh the intended outcome? The assessment of technological effects in the real world is much more difficult than the assessment of effects in an isolated laboratory. Interventions in nature are always experiments with nature, often resulting in irreversible consequences despite their aim to improve or to regenerate a contaminated environment. There is no consensus among environmental ethicists about the significance of the respective economic or ecological methods for managing environmental problems: in particular, ecology is, for many environmental ethicists, a 'weaker' science with little predictive power. They do not believe that it is possible to evaluate achieved effects in an adequate quantitative (financial) manner: for example, how can we estimate the costs of an extinguished insect species in the Amazonian rainforest? Is it possible and sensible to calculate such damage in a monetary form?

Even the question of what exactly the supposed environmental problem is and how urgent its solution, may require environmental ethical considerations. This question goes beyond pure technical aspects and relates to *normative* aspects. And normative questions are always also ethical questions. And what is 'good practice' in environmental management anyway? Before conducting a risk analysis we have to clarify, in a normative way, what a real risk is and whether there is a real risk in the given case (this is a question of risk perception). Using the same consideration we have to make a cost–benefit analysis: we have to know what values are involved and to what extent we are willing to pay for the conservation or re-creation of a polluted or damaged environment. How valuable is 'intact nature' for society? In addition, the ranking of the values involved has to be established before we take any measures. According to which normative criteria do we characterise 'values of nature'? In a utilitarian manner, related to its possible use for humans? Or deontologically, related to an inherent or intrinsic value of nature? At this point we have returned to those questions of environmental ethics that we have already touched on at the philosophical level.

Moreover, the question of what is a good aim for environmental protection or how we can recognise the success of a measure taken is often neither scientifically nor ethically easy to answer. Some environmental ethicists (coming from the concept of ecosystems) think that the balance of nature—its maintenance or restitution—should be the main goal of environment or nature protection. But it is often unclear when we can speak of a resilient and equilibrated system and how exactly we can determine the limits of the load capacity of an existing natural system (e.g. the global climate or a coral reef). Some could argue that certain disequilibria and instabilities that take place within nature are even desirable, because they are sources for change and evolution. Instabilities could even be the 'motor' of evolution; so long-term robust ecosystems are only exceptions within nature.

On the other hand, it is important for environmental ethicists to know which scientific and technical means (methods, tools, etc.) are at their disposal for purposes of environment protection. How far is it possible to determine the specific character of a given environmental problem and to assess the success of a measure taken in this field? It makes little sense, if we postulate ethically that all people have a right to clean drinking water but we do not have reliable methods to measure the quality of water and to determine and control threshold value for acceptable levels of chemicals. The fulfilment of ethical demands depends on the usability of methods of technical environment protection. Ethical norms often have to be translated into technical controllable norms (such as threshold values) to achieve practical relevance. Thus there is a controversy among environmental ethicists on how far environmental ethics should become scientific. In any case, modern environmental ethics does not ignore either the results of scientific ecology or the technological potentiality of practical environment protection.

As applied ethics, environmental ethics relies on the results of the empirical sciences; otherwise environmental ethics cannot formulate realistic demands and perspectives. Although, under an old philosophical principle, it is not allowable to deduce normative demands (duties) from being (existence) because ethical principles always precede empiricism, the practical success of environmental ethics depends on scientific knowledge: obviously it is not acceptable to decide only intuitively which the natural entities count as 'moral agents' to the 'moral community' and which do not. So we need a biological examination to recognise whether, for example, an eelworm has a nervous system and might be sentient and therefore—from a pathocentric perspective—worthy of protection. Also the question of what factors are responsible, and to what extent, for changes to the earth climate needs to be clarified by a detailed analysis of all processes playing a role in the climate change, before the true delinquents can be named and made accountable. But in the forefront of this analysis, environmental ethics can already point to possible risks and causes; moreover, environmental ethicists can demand scientific examinations and preach caution about current emissions. In this case they can refer to the obligation to maintain favourable life conditions for all people and other living beings. Confronted with a situation of unclear causation it is an ethical command to cut back the quantity of anthropogenic emissions for preventive reasons. Nevertheless environmental political and legal decisions need for their legitimisation not only ethical demands and doubts, but also scientific expertise and efficient means of technical environment protection.

Environmental ethics is undoubtedly of great importance in determining our relationship with nature and our behaviour towards it. In addition to internal struggles about what is the right position from a practical viewpoint, environmental ethics has to be based on the fundamental ideas of justice for all living beings worthy of protection and of ecological sustainability. Environmental ethics has the task of developing models (general orientations) in certain directions: (a) a model of sustainability, especially for resource ethics, (b) a model of species-appropriate handling for animal ethics, and (c) a model of intact nature in the area of ethics of nature. Environmental ethics provides the basis for environmental education. On the philosophical level environmental ethics offers reasons and arguments for distinct areas of environmental action on the political–legal and casuistic levels. Therefore environmental ethics is, and remains, a persistent challenge to modern society, because environmental ethics pleads emphatically for a cautious and ethical sensitive co-existence with nature.

Check your understanding of Lesson 3

1. For whom are philosophical considerations of environmental ethics important? And why?

2. What is the central problem in the debates of environmental ethicists?

3. In what sense could environment-ethical considerations influence eco-political decisions?

4. What role does the environmental consciousness play in the environment-oriented behaviour of individuals or society?

5. Give examples of environmental pollution and ecological damage in your own environment for which society should find solutions. And what could your own contribution be to this?

6. How important is it for society to preserve nature intact? Even if we have to give up many comforts?

7. Why should we humans place great value for ethical reasons on the protection of the environment and on the protection of species? To put it another way: If nature itself is ruthless towards animals and plants, why should we humans be kind to and thoughtful of non-human beings?

4

Main approaches to environmental ethics

Kees Vromans and Rainer Paslack

Central goals

The reader should: understand that environmental ethics questions the assumed moral supremacy of human beings over members of other species and seeks rational arguments to assign moral status to the natural environment and its non-human elements; understand the most important theories and their proponents and the anthropocentric and non-anthropocentric views of ethics (Lessons 1 and 2); and be able to clarify his or her own values by using the step-by-step scheme and the basic attitudes of humans towards nature and environment (Lesson 3).

4.1 Moral care for nature

Environmental ethics emerged as a new sub-discipline of philosophy in the early 1970s. Until that time philosophy had been questioning human actions towards human beings. Actions towards nature were dealt with in an anthropocentric way. Those actions were good or not good when the well-being of humans was at stake.

Since the 1970s traditional anthropocentrism has been challenged. In the first place, environmental ethics questions the assumed moral superiority of human beings to members of other species on earth. In the second place, it investigates the possibility of rational arguments assigning intrinsic value to the natural environment and its non-human elements.

4.2 Lesson 1: The anthropocentric view

Objectives

On completing this lesson, the reader will understand:
- What the term 'anthropocentric' means
- How the anthropocentric view of environmental ethics is philosophically founded
- That the anthropocentric approach to environmental ethics not only encompasses instrumental values, but also aesthetic and contemplative values

4.2.1 Different anthropocentric positions

The central ethical question is: Who or what belongs to the moral universe? In other words, to whom or what do we have direct moral obligations? Who or what has a dignity that must be respected? In this section we deal only with the anthropocentric view of the moral universe. We can state that the anthropocentric view of environmental ethics is totally human-centred. But also, within the tight boundaries of a moral universe seen as strictly human, there are different ways to answer our central question. Some of the most common answers are (after Krebs 1999: 19):

1. Only myself (egoism)

2. Myself, my family, and friends (small group egoism)

3. All people of my class (classism)

4. All citizens of my country (nationalism)

5. All people of my race (racism)

6. All people of my sex (sexism)

7. All living human beings (universalism of the present)

8. All living human beings and those of the past (universalism including the past)

9. All living human beings and those of the future (universalism including the future)

In the light of this sequence of nine steps, each of which expands the boundaries of the moral universe, a moral theory is anthropocentric if it opts for one of the positions between (1) and (9) within the boundaries of the moral universe and excludes all non-human beings from direct moral concern. From an amplified (physiocentric) perspective that also includes non-human beings in the moral universe, this anthropocentric position may seem as 'species egoism' or 'species-ism' (Singer 1975) or as a form of 'human chauvinism' (Routley and Routley 1979).

The above sequence presents a hierarchical structure, expanding the focus of anthropocentrism more and more. We cannot discuss all the different positions in detail here, but of special interest is the anthropocentric position number 9, because it includes the living humans not only of the present but also of the future. Indeed, what we do to nature today severely reduces the chances of future generations to lead good lives. If moral respect is respect for the good life of all others, it must include the good life of future generations. It is difficult to see what argument could be made against this approach. As Angelika Krebs says:

> Disregarding the good life of those who come after us, who have a different position in time, is parallel to disregarding the good life of those who have a different position in space, for instance people in the Third World. If the second is immoral, the first must be immoral too (Krebs 1999: 20).

We can't know exactly how the future will be and what future generations will need for their good life, but we can imagine some basic needs of the people to come; although we do not know their personal and culture-specific options for the good life, we know a lot about what are universally accessible basic options.

> They will, for example, want to be healthy and many of them will want to enjoy clear summer days. If we destroy the ozone layer and future generations must remain indoors to avoid skin cancer, how could this be morally right? (Krebs 1999: 20).

We can say that, because they will have existence, future generations have all the same moral rights that present generations have, including the right to life. Therefore an anthropocentric ethics has to claim that we have obligations to respect the environment for the sake of human well-being and prosperity in the present *and* in the future. Moreover, it is evident that the actions and policies that we contemporary humans undertake will have a great impact on the well-being of future individuals (see Gewirth 2001). Although there is a lack of reciprocity (because future generations cannot do anything for us in exchange for what we do for them), and a problem of knowledge (because we do not know exactly, who and how future people will be; see Parfit 1984), one can argue that our obligations lie with ensuring that we do not prevent future generations from meeting their basis needs (see Barry 1999). This, for instance, 'forces us to consider and appropriately revise our levels of pollution, resource depletion, climate change and population growth' (Cochrane 2007).

4.2.2 Instrumental value of nature

In the anthropocentric view animals, plants, ecosystems and the whole of nature have a 'value' only in relation to human beings and their interests. This is usually called 'instrumental value'. The most important consequence of this perspective with respect to the protection of environment and nature is that the only acceptable reason to conserve and cultivate nature is that the satisfaction of basic human needs—such as nourishing the body and maintaining health—depends on nature. Nature, especially in the form of natural resources, is a precondition for our biological and economic life; without nature human life is not possible.

In the anthropocentric view, nature (air, water, minerals, animals, plants, etc.) is necessary and valuable for human beings—but valuable *only in this sense*. There is no other reason for estimating nature, no value of nature for itself, but only in respect to human interests. And reluctance to use natural resources (animals, fossil fuels, minerals, etc.) can be justified only in respect to the needs and interests of contemporary humans or, at most, future generations.

So, for instance, the discussion of sustainable development frequently focuses on forms of resource management, with an emphasis on social justice and on the well-being of future generations of humans (see Palmer 2008: 18). Indeed, the most commonly cited definition of sustainable development, taken from *Our Common Future* (WCED 1987) is anthropocentric: 'Sustainable development is development that meets the needs of the present without compromising the ability of future generations to meet their own needs.'

From this viewpoint we do not need special environmental ethics, because all ethics are always *human* ethics. Values are both human-generated and human-focused. In principle, only humans have moral standing and are moral agents. In accordance with this very strict anthropocentric view we have to distinguish between, on the one hand, 'direct duties' to all beings with moral standing (i.e. all humans) and, on the other hand, 'indirect duties' to all beings (animals, plants, etc.) that humans (as moral agents) need for continuing their life responsibly, well-being. Nature is ethically valuable only in an indirect manner if, and only if, nature contributes to the needs and interests of humans. In consequence, we have to distinguish between 'value *in* nature' and 'value *of* nature' (Palmer 2008: 17): but only the second will be accepted by strict anthropocentrics such as the philosopher William Baxter, because for them there are no intrinsic values in nature itself. If we speak about the 'value *of* nature', then we only attribute to nature our own interests regarding nature. Without humans there would not be any 'natural' values.

But this strong anthropocentric view stands in sharp contrast to the intuitive feelings many people have towards nature: they esteem or love nature (natural beings such as plants and animals) for its own sake, not only for instrumental reasons. Wise or moderate anthropocentric philosophers concede that we can have more than instrumental interests in the environment and nature: they argue that it is not necessary for anthropocentric reasoning to emphasise only the pragmatic or utilitarian aspects of our interrelations with nature. Without leaving the anthropocentric position we can come into contact with nature in an aesthetic or contemplative way (more passive than active, enjoying rather than using in a technological sense).

4.2.3 Aesthetic and other values of nature

We have said that some less strict anthropocentrics concede that at least an aesthetic (or contemplative)[1] argument for protecting nature could be added to the instrumental view of nature; they base the need to conserve and cultivate nature on nature's sensual attractions for us, the pleasure we take, for instance, in breathing fresh mountain air.

Beyond a narrow instrumentalist perspective you can recognise nature's aesthetic and contemplative values. Such values resemble intrinsic values of nature, because they seem to be values of nature in itself, but nevertheless they are attributed by humans: they come into the world only through human beings and their aesthetic or contemplative practice. And hold in mind that aesthetic or contemplative values have another quality as moral or ethical values. For many people the term 'contemplative value' means not only that nature is an aesthetic resource for us, but also that nature is *absolutely* beautiful and sublime! Here the anthropocentric position goes over to an epistemic and ontological position (although not in a moral sense), examining the problem of how we can recognise nature in a metaphysical way.

However, someone can deny this ontological implication and argue that there is no independent aesthetic quality of nature in itself; that an aesthetic or contemplative value of nature only exists if a human being values nature's beauty and sublimity. You can consider for

1 'In aesthetic contemplation, we value entering into a relationship with the object that is not instrumentally guided. We allow ourselves to sink into the object so that it is experienced as if it were "speaking" to ourselves, as if it were "subject"-like or "autonomous" ' (Krebs 1999: 45).

yourself whether you think nature has *genuine* aesthetic worth or not. You might conduct a common thought experiment and ask: Would the last human being on earth commit a wrong if he or she destroyed nature? *If* it is wrong for the last person to destroy the whole planet, then non-humans must have value, perhaps even moral value in themselves!

Consider whether it is really a contradiction in itself to say that nature's aesthetic value is an 'aesthetic *intrinsic* value *for us*'. There may be aesthetic aspects of nature in itself that we also recognise as really existing, but that does not mean that we are free to decide what we regard as aesthetically pleasing in nature, because some of the qualities of nature necessarily have to be seen as aesthetic by anthropological reasons (based on the general human constitution).

> In finding it intrinsically valuable to contemplate something, we respond to qualities which inhere in it, its enormous size or power (giant redwood trees, waterfalls) or its structural complexity (bizarre rock formations), or its freedom from marks of instrumental human activity (the sea, the desert, the sky) (Krebs 1999: 46).

It may be that our inbuilt aesthetic perception is a prerequisite to experience the beauty and sublimity of nature, but this special relationship between nature and us is a fundamental (ontological *and* anthropological) trait both of us and the non-human natural world. Indeed, it is necessary to have aesthetic consciousness to experience nature as beauty, but nevertheless nature is beautiful in itself, and we possess an innate disposition to feel nature's beauty! These are complex philosophical questions that are not easy to answer, and this provides an opportunity to discuss the problem of the intrinsic values of nature from a more general perspective.

If one does decide that nature has an intrinsic aesthetic value, this does not mean that a *moral* intrinsic value must also be ascribed to nature. From an anthropocentric perspective moral intrinsic values are internal to our moral culture (and never external). On the one hand, anthropocentric philosophers may accept aesthetic and contemplative values as intrinsic values of nature, but, on the other hand, they can deny that moral values of nature are intrinsic values of nature: for them moral values are always human-related values of using and enjoying natural resources or phenomena. But they may concede that the contemplation of nature is valuable for a good human life. In this sense (and only in this sense) in an anthropocentric view the aesthetic value of nature (which may be an intrinsic value) *contributes* to the morality of humankind, insofar as life as a *good* life is of moral importance. So aesthetic (intrinsic) values of nature contribute in an *indirect* manner to ethics, although aesthetic values in themselves are not genuine moral values. This is indeed a very intricate consideration, but a typical example of philosophical reasoning.

The point is that the anthropocentric position is not principally against emotions or feelings; it doesn't refer only to material interests in nature. Anthropocentric thinkers can share with non-anthropocentric ethicists the special positive feelings towards the natural environment in which human beings have lived for long periods of their lives, because these places provide feelings of familiarity and security. These are feelings of 'homeland'. The homeland usually contributes to the identity of those who live there. Understanding yourself in terms of a native landscape is a common form of expressing individuality (see Krebs 1999: 55). A feeling of alienation and mourning will arise in many people who return to places where they have lived in former times, and see, for example, that the trees in front of their childhood home have vanished, that the whole natural environment has changed radically. Anthropocentric philosophers can agree with the idea that nature should be conserved if it is part of the home of humans. So the anthropocentric view is compatible with a certain idealism and even romanticism (towards 'homeland').

An anthropocentric-oriented person can also have empathy and compassion for sentient animals, although denying that sentient animals have any moral intrinsic value in themselves. The desire to avoid pain and unhappiness for all living beings is not unusual in an anthropocentric. To have compassion for living beings that can feel pain and distress doesn't need a special ethical justification, because for most people this is self-evident. Even without moral respect for nature one can love nature and hold it in high esteem. The anthropocentric view is not the same as a cold and heartless view of nature. Anthropocentrics can appreciate, in principle, all natural phenomena and their integrity, although they are do not attribute to nature any moral intrinsic value.

Only if the anthropocentric position is restricted to a purely instrumental view of nature is it then associated with a cruel and strict materialistic view. 'Only someone who damages or destroys nature without good reasons, someone who leaves an empty Coca Cola can lying around in a field, or who steps on a beetle or a flower, which could easily have been avoided, vandalizes nature.' In contrast 'When workers on a construction site fell trees to make space for a new building, they obviously do not do anything which corrupts their character. They do not vandalize nature' (Krebs 1999: 58).

Intelligent and prudent anthropocentrics will not destroy the natural environment just because they want to protect the natural base of their own lives, but also because they wish to protect their own positive (aesthetic and empathic) feelings towards an intact nature. So, ultimately, the behaviour of an anthropocentric will not differ from that of a moderate non-anthropocentric who concedes nature has a moral intrinsic value.

Only in comparison to a more fundamental non-anthropocentric ethicist will the anthropocentric ethicist act differently: for example, killing a cockroach in the kitchen, something a radical non-anthropocentric would never do. For an anthropocentric ethicist a cockroach may have an ecological value (value in the sense of 'function'), in so far as nature is a complex interconnected system (what humans need for their healthy life), but not a moral value in itself. From the anthropocentric's perspective there is no reason not to kill an individual cockroach; no moral respect will hinder him or her from extinguishing this single animal. This marks a clear difference between a moderate anthropocentric view and a radical non-anthropocentric view of nature. Nevertheless, as we have seen, there are different possibilities of arguing for 'values *of* nature' in an anthropocentric manner—not only in an instrumental or materialistic way. On the other hand, there are good reasons to claim that anthropocentric ethics is too narrow-minded because it is too human-centred, and that not only humans belong to the moral universe.

4.3 **Lesson 2: The non-anthropocentric view**

Objectives

On completing this lesson, the reader will understand:

- That the non-anthropocentric view encompasses four main theories: pathocentrism, biocentrism, ecocentrism and holism
- The arguments put forward by the theories and their proponents

In this section we look at rational arguments for giving intrinsic value to the natural environment and its non-human contents. First, some of the meanings of 'intrinsic value' and some functions of the use of that concept will be explained. Second, we look at some main theories and their proponents within the non-anthropocentric view. Each of them gives an argument to widen the 'moral community' with non-human beings.

At this point it is also important to take into account what you learned in Chapter 2 about correct moral reasoning. You, on your own or in a group, have to establish what the moral problem is and what the facts are. At least, you have to agree on what you call facts. This isn't an easy task, but it is important to establish the facts first and then the values. Sometimes you will find that after some thought and discussion facts seem to be values.

Before looking at the four main theories it is important to know something about the meaning and the use of intrinsic value.

4.3.1 Intrinsic value

In this section we look at the opposite of instrumental value: intrinsic value. Wouter Achterberg, arguably one of the founding fathers of environmental ethics in The Netherlands (1994: 182-87), citing Taylor (1986), makes a distinction of three kinds of intrinsic value.[2]

2 It is important to note that intrinsic value 'gives' moral status but moral status is not the same as 'having' intrinsic value. Intrinsic value can have different meanings and use of the concept can have several different functions.

Intrinsic value means:

a. What is directly experienced, felt as satisfying, pleasant or of worth *in itself*: for example, pleasure and luck according to the classic hedonistic utilitarian

b. The value that is given by humans to places or objects with an aesthetic, historical, cultural or even sentimental meaning

c. Beings or entities have certain essential properties. Because of those properties they deserve moral consideration and maintaining an attitude of moral respect towards them is the proper thing to do

Achterberg continues that intrinsic value has several functions:

• It can be used to define the limits of the moral community. Deontology uses intrinsic value (c) above. Goal ethics (utilitarian) uses (a) above

• It can be used to make responsible choices between the interests of human beings and other beings or entities and choices between other beings. Therefore (b) especially and also (a) are adequate

In the first function it is all or nothing: something has an intrinsic value or not. In the second the intrinsic value can vary. The two functions do not exclude each other; what matters is the type of ethics or morality. There is a distinction between narrow and broad morality.

Achterberg (1994) presumes that environmental ethics is trying to expand narrow morality to take account of the relations between human beings and other organisms. When intrinsic value is used to justify that expansion, the concept of intrinsic value (c) above is essential.

Returning to the non-anthropocentric view, it can be presented in many ways. In this book the view is presented by four theories:

1. Pathocentrism

2. Biocentrism

3. Ecocentrism

4. Holism

deals with the question of which elements of nature ... are candidates for moral status and what is the ... that moral status. These arguments have been touched on ... r 2 in the discussion of the main ethical theories. Each theory has its proponents. Table 4.1 provides a schematic presentation of the four non-anthropocentric theories.[3]

Table 4.1 Schematic presentation of the non-anthropocentric view

Theory	Versions of the theory	Candidate	Argument	Proponent
Pathocentrism	Utilitarianism Consequentialism Sentientism	All creatures that can suffer. All creatures that are 'sentient'	The overall balance of pleasure over pain. An individual animal has moral status as far as the individual pain or pleasure is part of the total sum of pleasure or pain.	Peter Singer
	Deontology		Individual animals have moral status (inherent value) because they are a 'subject-of-a-life'	Tom Regan
Biocentrism	Deontology	All creatures that live	Organisms have moral status because they have intrinsic value. They have a good of their own and have welfare interests.	Paul Taylor
	Consequentialism		All living beings have moral status because they have a good of their own but there is a hierarchy. Some living beings have greater intrinsic value.	Robin Attfield

---

3 For further information see Wenz 2001; Attfield 2003: 31-65.

Theory	Versions of the theory	Candidate	Argument	Proponent
Ecocen- trism		All organisms including ecological systems	Human beings and all other organisms have moral status because they have the right to flourish	Arne Naess
Holism		All natural things	The whole ('land') has moral status	Aldo Leopold

4.3.2 The pathocentric theory

This theory says that making animals suffer is wrong. Not only human beings feel pleasure or pain; animals can too. Animals are equal to human beings; they are both sentient. Within sentientism there are writers with a consequentialist argument or with a deontological one.

Peter Singer (1993) is a utilitarian. Utilitarianism, one of the consequentialist theories, focuses on the balance of pleasure and pain. An action can affect the interests of sentient beings. The interests of all sentient beings, including the non-human ones, should be taken into account equally when assessing an action to be right or wrong.

Singer and other utilitarians argue that intrinsic value lies in the experience of pleasure or the satisfaction of interests rather than in the beings involved in that pleasure or satisfaction. For utilitarians such as Singer, non-sentient objects in the environment such as plant species, rivers, mountains and landscapes are of no intrinsic value and at most of only instrumental value to the satisfaction of sentient beings. The utilitarian calculation can lead to the conclusion that an action that causes harm to individual animals may be right because other interests outweigh those of the animal involved.

Tom Regan (1983) has a deontological ethical argument. He argues that some animals that he has defined as a 'subject-of-a-life' have intrinsic value, which he calls inherent value. To be a subject-of-a-life involves, among other things, having sense-perceptions, beliefs, desires, motives, memory, a sense of the future and a psychological identity over time. Being the 'subject-of-a-life' is a sufficient condition for having intrinsic value. These animals have the moral right to respectful treatment and should not be treated as a mere means to an end.

4.3.3 The biocentric theory

Some authors have extended concern for individual well-being further, arguing for the intrinsic value of organisms because each organism has a reason for being, or a purpose, that is inherently good, whether those organisms are capable of consciousness or not. Paul Taylor's version of this view (1986), which we might call biocentrism, is a deontological example. In contrast to sentience-centred philosophers, who argue why should we care about organisms if they don't care about themselves, the biocentrists say that if we can harm an organism's welfare interests it is morally considerable, regardless of whether or not it has conscious desires or wants (e.g. crushing the roots of a tree may not 'hurt' it but it does harm it, therefore it has a welfare interest we can protect).

Unlike Taylor's egalitarian and deontological biocentrism, Robin Attfield (2003: 43-46) argues for a hierarchical view that says while all beings that have their own good reason for being have intrinsic value, some of them (e.g. people) have greater intrinsic value. Attfield also endorses a form of consequentialism that takes into consideration, and attempts to balance, the many and possibly conflicting good of different living things.

4.3.4 The ecocentric theory

According to Achterberg (1994: 13), ecocentrism means that natural entities *ought* to have the freedom to flourish or to function apart from human interference. Ecocentrism admits the moral status of human beings *and* also of all other organisms. Moreover, nature at a higher level of organisation than individual organisms, for example, at the level of species and ecosystems, deserves moral respect and has intrinsic value. A proponent was Arne Naess, who taught that 'ecology should not be concerned with man's place in nature but with every part of nature on an equal basis, because the natural order has intrinsic value that transcends human values. Indeed, humans could only attain "realisation of the Self" as part of an entire ecosphere'.[4] However, ecocentrism doesn't go so far as holism in considering the 'whole' (Mother Earth).

4.3.5 The holistic theory

According to Achterberg (1994: 168-87) there are two possible ways to expand our moral care towards collective entities such as ecosystems. One of them is by cognitive adjustment. We have to have a certain perception of nature. We have to change our view of complex natural entities themselves and in relation to what we usually consider as organisms. One example of this ecocentric way is the land ethic of Aldo Leopold. It is not a philosophical theory, but it is very inspiring. The land ethic can be found in the last chapter of *A Sand County Almanac* (Leopold 1949).

According to Achterberg remarks of Leopold bear witness to ethical holism: the ecosystem (the land) as a whole has moral status. The core is:

- The land *is* a community of interdependent elements;

- The land *as* a community *and* the elements have to be treated with moral respect

- The land has a value far above its economic and instrumental value, a value in the philosophical sense, something like 'intrinsic value'

The central thesis of Leopold can be found in the following sentence:

> Examine each question [of land use] in terms of what is ethically and esthetically right, as well as what is economically expedient. A thing is right when it tends to preserve the integrity, stability, and beauty of the biotic community. It is wrong when it tends otherwise (Leopold 1949: 262).

So Leopold uses two metaphors: the land as community and the land as organism. The first emphasises the relative independence of

---

4 www.guardian.co.uk/environment/2009/jan/15/obituary-arne-naess, accessed 26 March 2012.

the elements of the ecosystem and their moral status. The second underlines the systematic cohesion: the ecosystem.

Achterberg (1994) distinguishes three kinds of holism to clarify Leopold's position: metaphysical, methodological and ethical holism.

Metaphysical holism proposes that the 'wholes' are as real as their parts. **Methodological holism** claims that to understand the whole, for example, the ecosystem, the knowledge of the parts, seen apart, on their own, is not enough. According to **ethical holism** some 'wholes' can deserve moral consideration, have moral status, just as some companies have a legal status apart from the legal status of the individual shareholders. So the ethical holism doesn't need the metaphysical and the methodological as a basis. For Achterberg (1994), Leopold's *A Sand County Almanac* shows ethical holism and possibly methodological holism, but not metaphysical holism.

4.4 Lesson 3: Ethical decision-making

Objectives

On completing this lesson, the reader will be able to:

- Find out more about the theories and their proponents
- Use this knowledge to clarify the reader's own values

You have now reached a key stage in working through this book. After looking at the history of ethics in general and the main concepts of environmental ethics in particular you are now at the point where you can start applying your knowledge to decisions on human behaviour towards nature and the environment.

4.4.1 Using the step-by-step-scheme

The step-by-step-scheme introduced in Chapter 2 is one way to apply ethics to a dilemma.

First, you have to gather the facts, and when you are discussing a situation with others, you have to agree on the facts. It is important to differentiate between facts and values. Say, for example, you have to make a decision about the genetic modification of animals or plants. Under what circumstances can genetic modification be a good thing? Start by gathering the facts on genetic modification. What is the human action involved? To keep it simple, we agree on the facts that genetic modification is a human action towards animals or plants that introduces into the genes of animal or plant 'X' genetic material of living being 'Y'. That genetic material encodes with a quality of living being 'Y' that we (humans) want to be expressed in the genes of animal or plant 'X'. We want to alter 'X' for some purpose. What is that purpose? There can be different goals: for example, a medical improvement—by introducing human genetics information, the animal or plant can make building materials for a medicine that stops bleeding, a serious medical problem.

Case study 4.1 **Using cow's milk to produce essential drugs for humans**

Let us look at the genetic modification of cows.[5]

You have to decide whether the modification described in Step 1 is good or bad.

What are the pros and cons?

How can ethics and its main theories help you?

How can the positions of the environmental philosophers clarify your values?

Let us follow the step-by-step scheme of Chapter 2. But before we do, you have to say what your ethical position is. What do you think is important? What is your value? What is your norm? This is also an important part of correct ethical reasoning. An example might be: 'all suffering has to be eliminated'.

---

5 Information on the topic of genetic modification can be found in videos on YouTube, e.g. www. youtube. com/watch?v=Zzh5TVXaAr4 (accessed 20 March 2012).

Step 1: Description and analysis

Genetic modification is when a human takes some DNA from one species and inserts it into the DNA (sequence) of another species.[6] The modification is successful when the new bit of DNA is 'expressed' in the host species. That means that the host species will use the gene and benefits from it. In this case, a cow is given the human gene responsible for the clotting of blood and produces large quantities of milk with a protein that encourages blood clotting. The protein will be extracted from the milk to be used in medicine for people suffering from haemophilia and other blood-clotting disorders).

How many people suffer from haemophilia and how much human blood has to be donated to extract the genes for the medicine?

To genetically modify the cow you need to start experimental research. The outcome isn't sure, but in theory it can be done. When the human genetics information expresses itself in the milk of the cow, you only need to milk the cow so you will no longer need large quantities of human blood.

The experiments have to lead to just *one* cow being changed genetically. But of course you need several to do the experiments. The cows may suffer in the experiments. In the end the modified cow will not differ very much from other cows. Only her genes will have changed. Will it be possible for the cow to produce offspring with the same genetic information, or will a bull also be required?

To do the experiment according to scientific standards you need 20 cows. They have to be taken care of extremely well because any discomfort for them has a disastrous influence on the outcome of the experiments. The cows have to be operated on but not killed to know whether the experiment is successful.

Step 2: Assessment

For the sake of argument, let us suppose you reduce the weighing of interests to: 'It can help a lot of people and only 20 cows have to suffer a little.'

Based on your value or norm you decide whether or not the experiments are allowed. Earlier we took as an example of an ethical, moral presupposition 'all suffering has to be eliminated'. On that basis you would make the ethical decision that the experiments are allowed.

The second step is **assessment**. You assess your decision. You

6 We will give just a brief description here. In a classroom situation a case may be presented by text and/or by video.

evaluate your value or norm against those of the main theories and philosophers. Based on the knowledge so far, you can assess that decision by answering some questions:

First, you can answer the question of whether the case is an ethical dilemma based on the five criteria for calling a dilemma an ethical one (see Chapter 2, Lesson 2).

Second, if the answer is 'yes', you can take a closer look at the arguments that are relevant to your decision. For the sake of argument, the ethical presupposition is 'all suffering has to be eliminated'. Is this a teleological or deontological presupposition? It isn't easy—ethics never is. There are always questions to be asked. What do you mean by 'all suffering'? All *human* suffering?

That could make you someone who looks at the consequences of human actions towards human beings. Utilitarianism is one of the main teleological theories. Historically, the classical utilitarians, Bentham and Mill, identified the good with pleasure and also held that we ought to, bring about 'the greatest amount of good for the greatest number'. Utilitarianism is impartial and agent-neutral; everyone's happiness carries the same weight. So you decide that the human good has to be maximised. You are in favour of the genetic modification.

In environmental ethics the discussion on the difference between humans and other beings is relevant. Are human pleasures more important than those of animals? If there is a difference, what makes that difference? Are intellectual pleasures better than others, as Mill claims?

From Singer's utilitarian position the criterion for moral standing is sentientism. All, and only, sentient beings that can feel pleasure and pain are moral relevant. They have preferences that can be satisfied or frustrated. They can be affected by human actions. Singer believes that only vertebrate animals (with an internal bone skeleton) are sentient. A key Singer principle is the equal consideration of interests (Singer 1993): identical interests must be given equal moral weight. The type of being doesn't matter. So you have to give equal moral weight to the pleasure and the pain of the human beings and of the cows. In this case the number of human beings outweighs the number of cows.

Another possibility is that you consider your presupposition as a deontological one. The consequences of human actions aren't relevant. Human actions have to follow rules. You have a duty to act according to norms or principles. 'All suffering has to be eliminated' can be a rule, even a principle. Kant is the godfather of deontology, so let us use his thinking to see whether your rule stands. Is it a practical rule or an absolute norm, a principle?

When people ask themselves what they ought to do, they formulate a practical rule. Kant calls that practical rule a maxim. A categorical imperative denotes 'an absolute, unconditional requirement that asserts its authority in all circumstances, both required and justified as an end in itself'.[7]

Your maxim has to meet three criteria to become an absolute norm, a principle. You have a duty to act according to that norm, principle. So when you want your practical rule 'all suffering has to be eliminated' to be a universal law, when it treats humanity as an end and when you act as a true member of the moral community, your practical rule can be seen as a norm, a principle. You have to eliminate all suffering (of human beings).

The ethics of Kant are challenged by environmental ethics and by Tom Regan's deontological rights view. (Regan also challenges the utilitarian view of Singer.) According to Regan (1983) the kinds of act, not the consequences, make them right or wrong. Right acts treat individuals as an end in themselves. All individual 'experiencing subjects-of-a-life' have inherent value and have the right not to be treated as a means to an end. The criterion of moral status for is being an experiencing subject-of-a-life, which is not the same as simply being alive but:

> a conscious creature having a welfare that has importance to it; wants and prefers things, believes and feels things, recalls and expects things, has ends of its own, can be satisfied or frustrated; all these make a difference to the quality of the life as lived/experienced. Some animals are experiencing subjects-of-a-life and thus have moral standing and inherent value for the same reasons that humans do (Hettinger 2005 on Regan's views).

If you agree with Regan, you have to give moral status to the cows. You have to take into account that they are experiencing subjects-of-a-life and as such any experimentation for genetic modification has to be considered as violating their rights not to be treated as a means to an end.

So far we have only considered human actions towards animals. Only two main theories have been explained and challenged by two philosophers on animal ethics. You can extend the argument by looking at cases that challenge human actions towards all the other elements of nature and environment.

---

7 en. wikipedia. org/wiki/Categorical_imperative, accessed 20 March 2012.

Step 3: Justification

It is easy to confirm what kinds of argument have determined your final decision.

The question of what view of humans and society forms the basis of your choice brings us to basic attitudes of humans towards nature.

4.4.2 Using basic attitudes

A second way to assess your ethical decision is to look at the basic attitudes towards nature. There are at least four, which Zweers (1995) expands to six. Basic attitudes can be used to assess an ethical decision and to present a norm to human actions towards nature and environment. In this section we explain what a basic attitude is, what the six are and how to use them.

According to Zweers (1994) environmental philosophy deals with systematic and critical refection on the philosophical aspects of environmental problems, the environmental crisis. Originally environmental problems were seen as scientific problems. In the second phase they are also or merely considered as social problems. They have to do with the way the institutions of society, such as economics, education and science, are organised. Even the organisation of the human relationships is important.

The philosophical analysis can be regarded as the third phase of the diagnosis and the solution of the environmental crisis. In the third phase there is awareness that the fundamental character of the environmental crisis has to do with how people see life and society, with their norms and values. The basic attitude of human beings towards nature and environment is important to the diagnosis and the solution of the environmental crisis.

A basic attitude has to do with the way humans see themselves, nature and the relation between human beings and nature and environment. To understand the basic attitudes and to change them, it is also important to find the roots, to look into the history of each attitude[8].

Zweers (1995) distinguishes six basic attitudes:

1. The despot (tyrant, master)

2. The enlightened despot

3. The steward

4. The partner

5. The participant

6. Unity

The first three attitudes are characterised by the view that nature has only instrumental value to human beings, although the basic attitude of the steward has some notion of moral care towards nature. With the basic attitude of the partner the view that nature has some value in itself, some intrinsic value, is introduced. Looking at all the attitudes it is possible to draw up a scheme as shown in Figure 4. 1.

You can use the basic attitudes to decide what you ought to do and to analyse human actions towards nature and the environment. You can change your attitude to one that gives more (or less) intrinsic value to nature and environment. A useful exercise might be to analyse documents such as a company's declarations on environmental care. Always compare what these documents say with the actual practice (what does the annual report say?). There is a Dutch proverb 'Paper sometimes is patient', meaning that you can write what you want, but it doesn't mean it is actually going to happen.

Another example is taken from a Dutch philosopher, Kockelkoren (1993), who identifies four positions for comparing different levels of genetic engineering of plants. He makes a distinction between the goals of the genetic engineering, the types of genetic engineering and the effects on the plants. The positions are:

---

8 One famous and probably the earliest example of a study of the history of basic attitudes is Lynn Townsend White, Jr's essay 'The Historical Roots of Our Ecologic Crisis' (1967).

- YES

- YES, on condition that

- NO, unless

- NO

The basic attitudes can be found in many documents from the Dutch government and in documents advising that government.

You can also ask yourself what *your* basic attitude ought to be, looking at yourself, at nature and at your actions towards nature. You can use the basic attitude as a tool to analyse your actions. Depending on the outcome and your evaluation of the basic attitude you find, you can change it.

Companies and environmental consultants can do the same. Analyse the plans and the actions. Evaluate whether the basic attitude is what the company wants and change it when another basic attitude is more appropriate. Zweers (1995) pleads for a move towards participating with nature.

Figure 4.1 **A scheme showing six basic attitudes**

Source: author's own

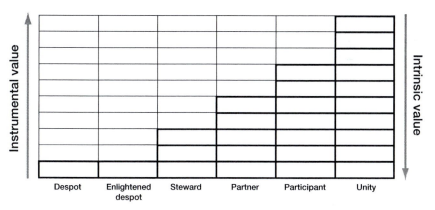

Check your understanding of all Chapter 4 lessons

1. What is the main interest of environmental ethics?
2. What is the difference between the anthropocentric and non-anthropocentric approaches?
3. What are the main theories within both views?
4. Who are the proponents of those theories?
5. What kinds of value are reasonable for the anthropocentric approach?
6. What are the arguments they put forward to assign moral status to non-human beings?
7. Can you give another example of human action towards nature and environment that meets the five criteria that make it an ethical problem?
8. Use the step-by-step scheme to analyse and to assess your ethical position regarding that problem? Do your values or norms stand when you confront them with the main theories?
9. What is your basic attitude towards nature and the environment?

5

The need for political and legal regulation

Rainer Paslack and Jürgen W. Simon

Central goals

The reader should understand how environmental issues can be regulated by law and politics, and how environmental ethics can contribute to this task; why political–legal regulation is needed (Lesson 1); the principles of political–legal measures (Lesson 2); and the instruments that regulate environmental behaviour (Lesson 3).

5.1 **Lesson 1: Why we need political–legal regulation**

Objectives

On completing this lesson, the reader will be able to:

- Understand what defines environmental politics and law and what are their goals and responsibilities
- Describe the different areas and issues for which environmental law is responsible
- Discuss generally the contribution of environmental ethics to the task of regulation of environmental questions by the state

Peaceful co-existence in modern societies requires political negotiation between conflicting interests and therefore needs a reliable and consistent legal order. The law is at the same time both a result and a condition of legitimate political action. Applied law is always influenced by the dominant moral values of a society. Most of all, the law provides the foundation for the decision or arbitration of cases, in which parties with different claims run up against each other.

This applies to conflicting or hazardous claims for the use of natural resources as well as to the treatment of non-human beings. Therefore in the 20th century a separate environmental legislation was established. This legislation takes account of the growing extent of societal intrusion into nature. As the environment becomes a scarce good, which many societal protagonists compete to utilise, while the natural habitats of plants and animals (and therefore themselves) are in danger of extinction because of the expansion of civilisation, politics and law are increasingly asked to protect nature from exhaustive cultivation, blight and destruction.

The mandate for a more efficient policy on the natural world and ecology is owed not least to growing public ecological awareness and an increasing appreciation of animals and plants for their own sake. Natural and environmental protection becomes a public duty, which is to be considered equally as important as the promotion of the economy or the attainment of social justice. As a result, environmental law increasingly rates highly within the legal system. And with the establishment of environmental law, environmental ethics is valorised as well, as environment ethical values are incorporated in the formulation of environmental law. From now on, the enforcement of environmental ethical demands in modern society is bound to the embodiment and effectiveness of environmental law.

Meanwhile, there are countless regulations that are either directly of an environmental nature or at least co-determined by environmental legal considerations and provisions: for example,

- The determination of critical values for emissions or fishing stocks

- The allocation of water licences

- The release of areas for development or agriculture

- Permission for constructing dams, bridges or airports or for altering river courses (canalisation), installing waste disposal sites, establishing industries or energy generation

Almost all human activities that encroach in some way on the environment or the ecosystem have the potential to raise environmental legal questions and require environmental legal regulations.

In general, political–legal regulation or environmental law is an important tool for the protection of the environment in accordance with economics and social life. It is a complex and interlocking body of statutes, common law, treaties, conventions, regulations and policies that, very broadly, operate to regulate the interaction of humanity and the rest of the biophysical or natural environment. The purpose of all legal regulation on the protection of environment is the reduction or minimisation of the impacts of human activity, both on the natural environment for its own sake and on humanity itself.

The most important areas environmental law has deal with are, among others: aid quality, water quality, global climate change, agriculture, biodiversity, species protection, pesticides and hazardous chemicals, waste management, remediation of contaminated land and sustainable development.

Environmental law is influenced by principles of environmentalism such as scientific ecology, responsibility for nature and the concept of sustainability. Insofar as environment protection is a public and state goal, it is based on several environmental political principles, which we will introduce later in this chapter, especially in Lesson 5.2.

But first some systematic directions to this branch of law should be given. The legal norms and rules can be divided into general and special environmental regulations. **General regulations for environmental protection** are not assigned to a special field, but are applicable across all sectors. **Special regulations for environmental protection** are differentiated according to the object of protection or the kind of measure. For the object of protection the legal orientation can be:

- **Media-related** for the protection of different environmental media (such as soil, water and air)

- **Causal** for the protection of the environment against hazardous emissions or substances

- **Vital** for the direct protection of animals and plants

In regard to the different kinds of measure, the environmental law can be related to:

- **Facilities** (serving a function, e.g. for air pollution control, radiation protection or energy saving)

- **Substances** (protection against hazardous chemicals, waste avoidance or waste disposal)

- **Areas** (for water pollution control, rural conservation or soil conservation)

Because no environmental code exists in which all relevant subjects of environmental protection are covered in an integrated manner, different branches of law are affected by environmental legal regulations: criminal law (or environmental criminal law), under which environmentally harmful behaviour becomes a punishable offence; and civil law, under which entitlement for compensation for ecological damage is regulated.

Environmental law holds numerous instruments through which the goals of environmental protection can be achieved and environmental political specifications can be efficiently implemented. The array of instruments includes especially:

- **Instruments for environmental planning** (primarily for the protection of resources or for the prevention of ecological risks)

- **Instruments for the direct control of behaviour** (prohibitions, orders and certain obligations for protagonists with relevance to the environment)

- **Instruments for the indirect control of behaviour** (influence on the motivation of protagonists with relevance to the environment)

In Section 5.3 we will expand on these instruments. First, however, we will turn to the principles that are (or should be) the basis for any ecological legislation; these are the organising principles to which the environmental law of the European Union and in general of all nations always refer.

Check your understanding of Lesson 1

1. In general, what is political–legal regulation necessary for?
2. What can environmental ethics contribute to environmental politics and law?
3. Discuss examples of what environmental law is needed for in particular.
4. To what areas and issues of environmental protection is environmental law assigned?
5. What are the most important goals and means of environmental law?

5.2 **Lesson 2: Principles for political and legal measures**

Objectives

On completing this lesson, the reader will be able to:
- Distinguish and explain the principles guiding environmental law both in a national and an international frame
- Understand the meaning of 'environmental sustainability' and 'sustainable development' in the context of nature protection

Serious and substantial environmental law has to be guided by some high-ranking principles. For many national regulations in the field of environmental law within the European Union (e.g. in Germany), four basic principles are the basis for all processes of environmental law-making: the precautionary principle, the polluter-pays principle, the principle of sustainable development (concerning the integration of environmental protection and economic development) and the cooperation principle. Other principles are often mentioned, which complete the four main principles or define them in a particular way. Some examples are:

- Environmental procedural rights
- Common but differentiated responsibilities
- International and intergenerational equity
- Common concern of humankind
- Common heritage

In this chapter we will focus on the four most important principles.

5.2.1 Precautionary principle

In its origin, the precautionary principle is rather a political than a philosophical principle and was first introduced as '*Vorsorgeprinzip*' (principle of precaution) in the German-speaking area. It was incorporated into several national legal texts and international treaties or declarations. A good definition was given by Per Sandin *et al.* (2002: 288): 'The basic message of the precautionary principle is that on some occasions, measures against a possible hazard should be taken even if the available evidence does not suffice to treat the existence of that hazard as a scientific fact.' It can therefore be stated that the precautionary principle is based on hazard detection and scientific uncertainty. As a consequence, the burden of proof (that an action might cause severe harm to the public or the environment) falls on those who plead for measures to prevent such a harm (see also Raffensperger and Tickner 1999). Whenever one can anticipate plausible harm for society or the environment, the precautionary principle should be applied. But often it is not clear whether a planned action will cause harm to the public or the environment or not, because the possible impact of human actions on the environment or human health often depends on the dynamics of complex systems, so the real consequences of actions may be unpredictable. Therefore further scientific research is required—but also caution if a current action intervenes in complex (human or natural) systems.

Nowadays the precautionary principle is incorporated into many European and international contracts and treaties. In its 1976 Report on the Environment, for example, the German Federal Government describes the precautionary principle as follows:

> Environmental policy is not limited to averting imminent danger and remedying damage that has already occurred. Precautionary environmental policy furthermore demands that the natural environment be protected and treated with care. The precautionary principle is embodied in a number of environmental provisions, and also involves resource conservation in addition to risk precaution (German Federal Government 1976).

The precautionary principle is especially important in legal regulations and decisions concerning potential risks to public health, such as the marketing of genetically modified foods, the use of growth hormones in cattle raising, or measures to prevent 'mad cow' disease.

Nevertheless, in real cases the policy-makers often have to struggle with a lack of valid scientific information or with irreducible conflicts between the interests of different stakeholders. Sometimes it is very difficult to estimate or assess the potential harm and to find an acceptable political compromise. But anyway, rigorous application of the precautionary principle should be avoided when there is insufficient knowledge of whether there is a real potential risk from an innovative product or an activity or not. In this case the principle could be taken immoderately as an absolute ban on all actions (see Van den Belt 2003), which could stall all technological innovation and progress.

5.2.2 Polluter-pays principle (versus community-pays principle)

'The polluter-pays principle states that the one causing environmental impact is principally held responsible—materially and financially—for protecting the environment and is required to prevent, correct, or financially compensate such impact' (Knopp 2008: 7). But a problem arises in cases of inherited pollution where the responsible parties often cannot be held liable and—if no other party can be held responsible—the general public must bear the cost. In such cases the polluter-pays principle would be replaced by the community-pays principle.

In environmental law, the polluter-pays principle is enacted to make the party responsible for producing pollution responsible for paying for the damage done to the natural environment. It is regarded as a general custom because of the strong support it has received in most Organisation for Economic Co-operation and Development (OECD) and European Community (EC) countries. In international environmental law it is mentioned in Principle 16 of the Rio Declaration on Environment and Development (1992).[1]

The polluter-pays principle is an important element of environmental policy and influences: for example, political measures for reducing greenhouse gas emissions. Often this principle will be applied as the so-called 'extended polluter responsibility' (EPR). This

---

1 The text of the declaration is available at United Nations Environment Programme: www.unep.org/Documents.Multilingual/Default.asp?documentid =78&articleid=1163, accessed 13 March 2012.

concept was probably first formulated by the Swedish government in 1975. For instance, EPR can help to shift the responsibility for dealing with waste from governments and taxpayers to the real producers of the waste. OECD defines EPR as:

> a concept where manufacturers and importers of products should bear a significant degree of responsibility for the environmental impacts of their products throughout the product life-cycle, including upstream impacts inherent in the selection of materials for the products, impacts from manufacturers' production process itself, and downstream impacts from the use and disposal of the products. Producers accept their responsibility when designing their products to minimise life-cycle environmental impacts, and when accepting legal, physical or socio-economic responsibility for environmental impacts that cannot be eliminated by design.[2]

5.2.3 The principle of sustainability (sustainable development)

Another important principle is the principle of sustainable development, which may be viewed as an instance of applying the precautionary principle to resources. This principle is a pattern of resource use that aims to meet human needs while preserving the environment so that these needs can be met not only in the present, but also for future generations. For the first time, the term 'sustainable development' was used by the Brundtland Commission in 1987, which has given the most famous definition of sustainable development as development that 'meets the needs of the present without compromising the ability of future generations to meet their own needs' (United Nations 1987).

The term 'sustainable development' seeks to combine the resources and processes of natural systems with the human needs and economic activities of social systems. Already in the 1970s the term 'sustainability' had been used for an economy 'in equilibrium with basic

2   OECD factsheet on EPR: www. oecd. org/document/53/0, 3343,en_2649_343 95_37284725_1_1_11,00.html, accessed 1 March 2012.

ecological support systems' (Stivers 1976). On the base of the idea of sustainability and according to the alarming theses of *The Limits to Growth* (Meadows *et al.* 1972), many ecologists tried to create the new concept of a 'steady state economy' (Daly 1973), especially with respect to environmental concerns. In this context, 'sustainable development' does not refer solely to environmental issues, but also takes into account social and economic considerations: the resolving of conflicts between different competing goals and stakeholders, and the harmonising of economic growth and social welfare with environmental quality. The concept of sustainable development—*both* of nature and society—points out that the survival of humankind depends essentially on the survival of nature (or the natural environment), because economic and socio-cultural welfare is directly coupled with the welfare of nature—resources, plants, animals, etc. Ultimately, the exploitation and degradation of nature can result in the inability to maintain human life and even in the extinction of humankind. The theory of sustainable development is therefore based on the assumption that societies have to manage three forms of non-substitutable capital: economic, social and natural capital (for further information see Dyllick and Hockerts 2002; Daly 1973, 1991). It may be that we can find ways to replace some natural resources, but it is unlikely that we will ever be able to replace the services provided by the ecosystem: for example, to protect us against dangerous cosmic radiation with an intact ozone layer, or to supply us with sufficient oxygen as the tropical forests or the algae of the oceans do. The multi-functionality of many natural resources and also biodiversity are irreplaceable. Moreover, the deterioration of natural resources and the loss of natural services (e.g. the absorption of nutrients by a lake) are often irreversible processes—like the loss of ethnic and cultural diversity (e.g. indigenous languages). Therefore only sustainable development can secure both: the protection of a functional intact environment and the survival and welfare of human beings.

5.2.4 Cooperation principle

'The cooperation principle underscores that environmental protection is the responsibility of all of society and not just of the state: accordingly, all parts of society and the state are called on to cooperate' (Knopp 2008: 49). The cooperation principle is the weakest of the four environmental principles, and it can hardly be considered as satisfying the requirements demanded of a guiding principle of law.

5.2.5 Other principles

Apart from the four basic principles, there are a number of others guiding national and international environmental law, such as the 'grandfathering principle'[3] or the 'principle that action may not result in a significant deterioration of environmental conditions' (Knopp 2008: 49). Last but not least, we should also mention the principle of transboundary environmental protection: this principle mirrors the insight that environmental problems do not stop at national borders. For instance, this principle underpins much of the Water Framework Directive of the European Union where it covers the transboundary management of water resources in natural river basins.

National as well as international environmental law are often based on the above called principles, especially the transboundary principle. This is important, because many environmental problems are border-crossing problems: for example, climate change, seawater and air pollution.

International environmental law is the body of international law that concerns the protection of the global environment. Originally associated with the principle that says that states must not permit the use of their territory in such a way as to injure the territory of other states, international environmental law has since been expanded by a plethora of legally binding international agreements. These encompass a wide variety of areas that have potential issues, from terrestrial, marine and atmospheric pollution through to wildlife and biodiversity protection.

The key constitutional moments in the development of international environmental law are:

3 Müller writes: 'The grandfathering principle defines the distribution of emission rights according to the emission distribution in a base year before emission restrictions came into force. In a next step it restricts the emission rights proportionally to this base year structure, usually some percent less than in the base year' (Müller 2005: 3, footnote 2).

- The 1972 United Nations Convention on the Human Environment (UNCHE), held in Stockholm, Sweden

- Publication of the 1987 Brundtland Report, *Our Common Future*, which coined the phrase 'sustainable development'

- The 1992 United Nations Conference on Environment and Development (UNCED), known as the Earth Summit, held in Rio de Janeiro, Brazil

As a core principle of the environmental law of nations it was determined at the Stockholm conference in 1972 that states are entitled to exploit their own resources, but that it is also their responsibility to ensure that actions originating in their territory are not causing any damage to the environment of other states. This policy is known today as 'customary international law'. This law includes all norms and rules that countries follow as a matter of custom, and they are so prevalent that they bind all states in the world. When a principle becomes customary law is not always clear-cut and states not wishing to be bound put forward many counter-arguments.

Examples of customary international law relevant to the environment include:

- The duty to warn other states promptly about emergencies of an environmental nature and environmental damage to which another state or states may be exposed

- Principle 21 of the Stockholm Declaration ('good neighbourliness')[4]

However an obligation of the state to take certain actions (for example, a prohibition of any transboundary damages to the environment) cannot be deduced from customary international law; at most there

---

4 Principle 21 of the UNCHE Stockholm Declaration (1972): 'States have, in accordance with the Charter of the United Nations and the principles of international law, the sovereign right to exploit their own resources pursuant to their own environmental policies, and the responsibility to ensure that activities within their jurisdiction or control do not cause damage to the environment of other States or of areas beyond the limits of national jurisdiction.' See www.unep.org/Documents.Multilingual/Default.asp?documentid=97&a rticleid=1503, accessed 13 March 2012.

is an obligation to adhere to due diligence, which obtains generally between states (see Simonis 2003: 227). Nevertheless, we can proceed on the assumption that international environmental law will gain ever-increasing importance. This will ultimately depend on how fully the principles pronounced in the 1972 Stockholm Declaration will be implemented in cross-national stipulations. A special role in this process could also be played by the concept of 'the common concern of humankind', which has been confined so far to climate protection and biodiversity. And the United Nations Framework Convention on Climate Change (UNFCCC), the international treaty produced at the Earth Summit in 1992 could eventually mean that countries will take their obligations against global environmental problems more seri-ously—particularly with regard to North–South relations.

In Lesson 3 we will look at the various instruments that individual states can command to translate their environmental plans into action and to regulate or influence positively the behaviour of their citizens in their treatment of the environment.

Check your understanding of Lesson 2

1. What are the most important principles guiding environmental politics and law?
2. What is the use of the 'precautionary principle', and which are the main forms of this principle?
3. Discuss problems in the implementation of the polluter-pays principle
4. What is meant by 'responsible environmental sustainability' in the area of eco-politics?
5. In which situations is *international* environmental law required? When is it crucial to have an international environmental law?

5.3 **Lesson 3: Regulation of environmental behaviour**

Objectives

On completing this lesson, the reader will be able to:

- Estimate the importance of appropriate 'environmental behaviour' in terms of environmental law
- Discuss the differences between direct and indirect regulation of environmental behaviour
- Point out the applicability of the different instruments of environmental politics and law to regulate environmental behaviour

---

5.3.1 Instruments to enforce environmental policy (planning)

Environmental policy has developed in the industrialised countries primarily as a reaction to the highly intensive growth of the environment industry at the beginning of the 1970s into special government departments. At first policy confined itself mainly to the activity of the state. Over the years, however, more and more protagonists with any interests in the environment field (so-called 'stakeholders') are being called to account on environmental matters. In particular, the responsibility of the producer of (potential) environmental problems is becoming increasingly significant. There is also a need to exert eco-political goals and strategies in other departments: for example, in policy for energy, transport and industry, agriculture, and building and construction. 'Hard' eco-political instruments (such as laws and regulations) exist side by side with the 'soft' methods of behavioural control (such as educating engineers about environmental awareness).

Besides environmental law, environmental planning forms a central set of tools, to the extent that environmental policy tries to operate not only as a regulatory but also as a formative instrument. Environmental planning can be regarded as the development of sustainable environmental strategies to facilitate the achievement of regional or sectoral environment protection goals within a certain time-frame: for example, the reduction of CO_2 emissions by 25% within the next ten years. In the 1980s the implementation of national environmental plans in Denmark, The Netherlands and Finland played a pioneering role in this. We will, therefore, first expand on the possibilities of environmental planning.

To enforce environmental policy principles and objectives two instruments (according to Knopp 2008) are implemented in the legal framework of many states within the EU:

1. Different types of environmental planning

2. Different measures for regulating environmental behaviour

Environmental planning provides an important means of precautionary protection. Planning takes place as a multi-stage process, involving registering the current situation and forecasting future developments; moreover, it has to take into account possible conflicts of interest.

Plans can take the form of laws, statutory regulations, statutes, administrative regulations or administrative acts, each of which has different legal consequences. In addition, environmental planning may involve comprehensive planning or sectoral planning. Two forms of environmental planning are dominant:

- **Comprehensive planning.** The task of comprehensive planning is 'to determine, while exercising foresight, land use for residential, economic and leisure purposes for a certain area, irrespective of any specific project and not limited to any specific sector' (Knopp 2008: 51)

- **Sectoral planning.** By contrast, sectoral planning serves to establish environmental protection plans for specific sectors, chiefly landscape, clean air, noise abatement, water conservation and waste management, all of which require additional enforcement measures

Another important instrument for enforcing environmental policy demands is **environmental impact assessment** (EIA). The primary objective of this instrument is 'to inform the administration comprehensively and in good time about the environmental impacts of environmentally significant projects' (Knopp 2008: 52). EIA is used to identify, describe and assess all of the direct and indirect impacts of a planned project on the environment, including ecological interactions, in good time, thus allowing precautionary measures to be taken across all media and sectors, and involving the public.

5.3.2 Instruments to regulate environmental behaviour

Environmental behaviour is perhaps the most important target for environmental policy and education. There are various instruments for regulating environmental behaviour, which can be distinguished as **direct** or **indirect** forms of regulation:

Direct regulation of behaviour

Direct regulation of behaviour pertains to legal measures designed to have an immediate affect environmental behaviour. The traditional instrument of this type is environmental regulatory law, 'which originates from police and regulatory law and generally punishes noncompliance by imposing sanctions' (Knopp 2008: 53). Accordingly, actions with adverse environmental impact are subject to administrative control, which is characterised by legal requirements of notification, registration, licensing, authorisation, approval and other procedures of granting permission to engage in such activity. In addition, direct regulation is also exercised by means of expressly prohibiting or requiring certain behaviour by law.

The following forms or instruments of direct regulation of behaviour exist:

- **Absolute legal bans** (e.g. in Germany under the Federal Nature Protection Act 2002, §§23[2], 42[1,2]), directly forbid certain behaviour with adverse impact on the environment. However, legislators only rarely employ measures of this type

- By contrast **permission procedures** are the key instrument in current environmental regulatory law in many European states. Projects subject to permission are strictly prohibited without permission. 'Erecting or operating an installation of environmental significance, using environmental media, or producing and distributing certain products may all be subject to permission' (Knopp 2008: 54). Thus a permit is a constitutive administrative act in that it grants the applicant the right of lawfully engaging in an otherwise prohibited activity

- Environmental law includes a number of so-called **environmental obligations**, of which **basic obligations** are of special significance. They impose certain obligations either on everyone or on a certain group of people. Normally, these basic obligations involve preventive and precautionary measures, most notably the conservation of resources (e.g. water or soil). Apart from those basic obligations, there are 'numerous **collateral obligations** that may benefit the environment, such as promotion and performance obligations, monitoring and protection obligations, obligations to cooperate and continuously disclose information, organisational obligations and obligations to tolerate certain actions' (Knopp 2008: 56)

Indirect regulation of behaviour

Indirect regulation of behaviour does not rely on norms mandating behaviour, but aims to influence motivation: incentives are provided for environmentally friendly behaviour while leaving discretion to the addressee. The means of indirect regulation behaviour notably include informational instruments, economic instruments, such as levies certificates and subsidies.

- **Information, appeals and warnings.** According to the German Environmental Information Act (1994), providing free access to environmental information is viewed as a means of sharpening the awareness of citizens and public authorities of the need for effectively protecting the environment. These means of raising environmental awareness range from political and moral appeals to warnings, recommendations and other forms of information, such as labels and product and usage information

- **Levies.** The most important means to indirectly regulate behaviour are environmental levies. 'They place a price tag on the use of the environment and leave it to market participants to decide if and how they will react based on their individual cost–benefit analyses' (Knopp 2008: 58). In practice, the inability to precisely affect behaviour via environmental levies can pose a problem. If they are set too low, polluters will opt for paying the levy instead of altering behaviour harmful to the environment. If levies are set too high, they may impede economic competitiveness. For instance, the following environmentally relevant charges are being levied in Germany in 2012:

- Waste-water charges
- Countervailing charges under nature conservation law and forest protection charges in various German States
- Water abstraction fees in some German States ('water penny')
- Waste transportation charges (consumer law)

Environmental levies may be imposed as taxes, fees and contributions for benefits incurred, and special levies.

- **Granting benefits to users of environmentally friendly products.** 'Benefits for use' refers to provisions that relax or lift general limitations imposed on the use of environmentally harmful products in the case of products that comply with standards that, although not required by law, are considered desirable, thus rendering such a product more environmentally friendly than others of the same kind. 'Although this instrument does not involve financial incentives in the medium and long term, changes in consumer behaviour may be expected that may lead to crowding environmentally more harmful products out of the market' (Knopp 2008: 60)

- **Subsidies.** Providing financial assistance is a form of indirect behaviour regulation. Subsidies are monetary or non-monetary benefits granted by the state, without any product or service being provided in return. Subsidies are generally viewed with scepticism, since they are considered to be prone to abuse and to place the cost burden of environmental protection on the general public. In the European Union there has been a tendency to cut back on environmental protection subsidies

- **Environmental certificates.** The idea of environmental certificates is based on a market-compatible form of quantity control by the state. Certificate-based schemes do not take prices as their starting point but define an admissible level for a certain future use of the environment in quantitative terms, leaving the formation of process up to the market. This instrument has been employed for climate protection under the **Kyoto Protocol**. The allocated emission allowances grant the holder the right to pollute the environment only to a certain extent. Should the holder pollute the environment to a lesser degree than permitted, the holder may sell the unused pollution allowances to another polluter. 'Enterprises may thus elect to either reduce emissions from their installations or to acquire additional emission allowances from other enterprises that have been able to reduce emissions at lower cost' (Knopp 2008: 61). Future experience will show whether this instrument will indeed prove successful in reducing greenhouse gas emissions

Economic instruments are gaining increasing significance as a complement to environmental regulatory law. There is no single answer to the question as to what is actually the 'proper' choice of instruments in order to achieve an adequate balance between various environmental user interests, the interests of affected neighbours, the interests of the general public and the protection of the environment. Legislators and administrations are thus ultimately compelled to rely on trial and error to reach an appropriate decision.

Check your understanding of Lesson 3

1. Why is environmental behaviour so important?
2. What can environmental regulation contribute to the improvement of environmental behaviour?
3. What forms of environmental planning are possible? Discuss examples from your own everyday life
4. Discuss the differences between direct and indirect regulation of environmental behaviour. Which instruments would you choose and why?

6

From environmental ethics to sustainable decision-making

Rob de Vrind

Central goals

The reader should understand the principles taken into consideration in sustainable decision-making (Lesson 1), understand how to use the step-by-step tool to help with sustainable decision-making (Lesson 2), and be aware of two methods of assessing the competing views of stakeholders (Lesson 3).

6.1 Lesson 1: Principles of sustainable development and cradle to cradle

In recent years we have begun to realise that environmental issues must be viewed in their entirety. As with all environmental issues, there are social, economic and ecological aspects and an optimum must be found for each aspect. Hence, nowadays the keynote for the

concept of sustainable development is one that considers **people,
profit** and **planet**—the three Ps—integrally.[1] Furthermore, a proper
assessment should also consider the (distant) future and the effects
on developing countries (see Fig. 6.1).

Figure 6.1 **Sustainable decisions should be based on people,
profit and planet (three Ps)**

Braungart and McDonough's **cradle-to-cradle** principle is also
receiving increasing attention (McDonough and Braungart 2002).
According to this concept, the new generation of products must not
contain any poisonous substances and all products must be fully

1 The three Ps are a succinct way of describing the triple bottom line, a phrase
  coined by John Elkington, the founder of British consultancy SustainAbility
  to represent social, economic and environmental concerns.

recyclable. The design of the product must allow easy separation of degradable and non-degradable materials. The degradable materials will enter the biosphere to become nutrients for nature. The non-degradable materials will be re-used in the technosphere. All processes must use energy from renewable sources. If we can achieve this, we can produce whatever we want, for a great many years to come. According to cradle to cradle, the principle of 'the polluter pays' should change to 'thou shalt not pollute'.

Check your understanding of Lesson 1

1. What are the two recent insights into current environmental issues?
2. On what environmental ethics do you base sustainable decision-making?
3. On what principles do you base sustainable decision-making?

6.2 Lesson 2: A step-by-step plan for sustainable decision-making

From what you have read so far you can now see how the step-by-step plan that has been discussed in Chapters 2 and 4 might be used for making sustainable decisions (see Fig. 6.2).

Step 1: Analysis

- Give a brief description of the situation. Examine the facts, and postpone your judgement
- Who is involved in the process?
- Step into the shoes of those people, and examine what their interests are with regard to people, profit and planet. Take the long-term consequences and the possible consequences for the developing world into consideration as well

Step 2: Assessment

- What solutions might the various stakeholders come up with?

- What are the pros and cons of the various solutions?

- What do the solutions have in common?

- What do constitutional principles imply (such as the precautionary principle, the polluter-pays principle and the principle of cooperation or good neighbourliness)?

- What do resource ethics, nature ethics and sustainable development ethics say?

- What do the principles of sustainable development (the three Ps) and cradle-to-cradle design say?

- Finally, come to a decision, reach a compromise and, if relevant, consider whether damage can be offset

Step 3: Justification

- Can you defend the decision of your choice?

- Would people who are considered a great moral example have come to the same decision?

- Had your friends or relatives been affected, would you have come to the same decision?

- Would you mind if the decision affected you personally?

- Is the decision in conflict with your own standards and values? What does your conscience tell you?

- Is the decision in conflict with law and legislation?

- Is the decision in conflict with the ethics of your occupation or profession, your institution or company?

Figure 6.2 **Sustainable decision-making finds an optimum between the three Ps and ethical views**

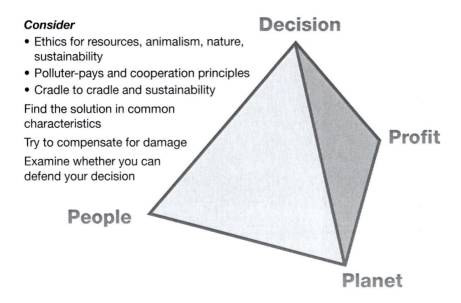

Consider
- Ethics for resources, animalism, nature, sustainability
- Polluter-pays and cooperation principles
- Cradle to cradle and sustainability

Find the solution in common characteristics

Try to compensate for damage

Examine whether you can defend your decision

Decision

Profit

People

Planet

We can illustrate the step-by-step process by reconsidering the case study (1.2) that appeared in Chapter 1.

Case study 6.1 **Dennis's dilemma (part 2)**

Dennis is an environmental engineer working in the textile industry. The factory discharges industrial waste-water into a lake adjacent to a tourist area. Dennis is responsible for monitoring discharges into water and air, and he compiles the reports for the Inspectorate for the Environment.

Measurements recently showed that the amount of dissolved particles and the chemical oxygen demand (COD) were slightly higher than allowed. Although the effect on people in the area is not very threatening, the fish stock in the lake may be affected. A solution to the problem will cost at least €100,000. The measures to be taken may even cost a few jobs. The General Manager has asked Dennis to adjust the figures slightly. In your opinion, how should Dennis react to this request?

The step-by-step plan

Step 1: Analysis

What are the facts?
The figures are slightly higher than the standard. Fish may be affected, but there is no danger for the population. Waste-water is discharged into a lake used by tourists. Dennis is aware of the facts. A solution is expensive (€100,000). The General Manager wants him to adjust the figures.

Who are the stakeholders?
The Ministry, Dennis (who draws up reports and monitors), the General Manager, the factory employees, the tourists, the community in the vicinity (and possibly the fish in the lake, or the entire surrounding ecosystem, or even the entire earth in general).

Step into the shoes of those stakeholders and examine what their interests are with respect to people, profit and planet. Take the long-term consequences and the possible consequences for the developing world into consideration as well.

The Ministry

People	A rule is a rule. Everybody must observe the rules. If we bend the rules, there could be serious consequences. We agreed these rules together
Profit	By not allowing exceptions, we ensure we do not have to spend huge amounts of money on water treatment and the cost of pollution-related illnesses
Planet	The rules serve to protect the environment
Solution	Set a deadline for the factory to solve the problem

Dennis

People	I want to keep my job. I want to do my job properly. And I should consider the other employees
Profit	If the company goes bankrupt, I will lose my job. The measures are expensive. The cost of delay may eventually be even higher
Planet	The fish will die. Through bioaccumulation, the hazardous material will eventually end up in human beings in a concentrated form
Solution	Set a deadline for a solution to the problem

The General Manager

People	I want to keep my staff (and myself) at work
Profit	The most important goal is to keep the factory in operation. I cannot afford the implementation of a cleaner process
Planet	If nobody is aware of it, we have no problem (yet)
Solution	Have Dennis adjust the figures and we will see what happens

The employees

People	We want to keep our jobs
Profit	The most important goal is to keep the factory in operation
Planet	If nobody is aware of it, we have no problem (yet)
Solution	Have Dennis adjust the figures and we shall see if the more ethical employees will head in a different direction

Tourists and the community in the vicinity of the factory

People	Work is important, but we like to live in a clean environment and we also need the tourists
Profit	The tourists bring in cash. We want to keep it that way
Planet	No fish will result in algal bloom resulting in poor swimming water quality, etc. Through bioaccumulation, the hazardous material will eventually end up with us
Solution	Set a deadline for the factory to solve the problem

Step 2: Assessment

- **What solutions might the various stakeholders come up with?** Some are suggested above.
    - What are the pros and cons of the various solutions?
    - What do the solutions have in common? Try to find a balance between the three Ps.
- **What do constitutional principles imply** (such as the principles of precaution, polluter pays and cooperation)?
    - **Polluter-pays.** If the company is eventually charged for cleaning up the pollution they caused, they will be even worse off.

- **Cooperation.** The polluted water flows downstream and may cause problems there.

- What do **resource ethics, nature ethics** and **sustainable development ethics** say?
  - According to **resource ethics** clean water must be conserved.
  - Based on **nature ethics**, the fish or the lake might have a vote as well. What gives humans the right to create misery for the fish, to undermine the ecosystems in the lake, and to decrease its biodiversity? What gives them the right to pollute the water, when nature relies on clean water? We do not know what the effects of prolonged exceeding of the standard are. By allowing the pollution, we violate the asset value of the fish that are poisoned, the ecosystems, nature and the entire earth. The fish were not included as stakeholders but in some ways they are; if they could vote, they would want the factory to stop dumping.
  - **Sustainability ethics.** If the pollution continues it will damage the water and eventually harm fish and people (tourists).

- What do the **principles of sustainable development** (the three Ps) and **cradle to cradle** say?
  - The principle of **sustainability** requires us to act in ways that will allow future generations to fulfil their needs. Future generations will want the benefits of tourism, good-quality swimming water, etc. Closing the factory is not a viable option because people's livelihoods depend on it.
  - The **cradle-to-cradle** principle says: look for non-hazardous production methods, based on renewable energy. That is the only way to sustainability.

- Finally, **come to a decision**, a compromise, and consider if the damage can be offset.
  - You need solutions with the smallest possible loss in the area of the three Ps.
  - It is often impossible to satisfy everybody.
  - One must find an area in which a collective solution can be found. Perhaps damage compensation can be arranged.

- **Solution.** Draw up a transitional arrangement to enable the factory to start manufacturing in an as environmentally clean way as soon as possible. If the business cannot afford the measures needed the factory will lose its licence and be forced to close.

Perhaps the community and tourist industry can contribute as well because it is to everyone's advantage to keep it going.

Step 3: Justification

If you opt for this solution, you can answer the following questions (Van den Herik and Winkler 2009):

- Can you defend the your decision? *Yes*
- Would people who are considered a great moral example have come to the same decision? *Yes*
- Had your friends or relatives been affected, would you have come to the same decision? *Yes*
- Would you mind if the decision affected you personally? *Yes*
- Is the decision in conflict with your own standards and values? What does your conscience tell you?
- Is the decision in conflict with law and legislation? *No*
- Is the decision in conflict with the ethics of your occupation or profession, your institution or company? *Yes, the company wanted you to adjust the figures, but that is not ethical*

Check your understanding of Lesson 2

1. Apply the step-by-step plan to other cases.

6.3 Lesson 3: Two methods for comparative assessment

To come to an ethical decision, the people, profit and planet arguments of the various stakeholders must be assessed. You can give all participants in the exercise the role of a specific stakeholder and then, in a kind of round-table discussion, have them discuss how a solution can be found. Hence, in Case study 6.1, the Ministry, the general manager of the factory, the environmental engineer, an employee of the factory and a representative of the community get round the table. Have them put arguments **against** one another.

Figure 6.3 **Six thinking hats**

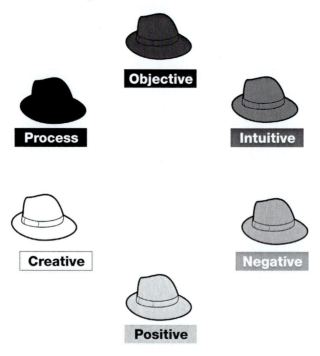

There is also a method to solve a problem **with** one another. This is the 'Six Thinking Hats' method (see Fig. 6.3), which is a tool to help you to look at decisions from different perspectives, forcing you to move outside your usual thinking style and get a more rounded view. Each hat has a different style of thinking: for example, the yellow hat represents 'helps you to think positively, the green hat helps you to develop creative solutions, etc. (See De Bono [1985] for more information on how to use this technique.)

Check your understanding of Lesson 3

1. What is the difference between the two methods assessing the stakeholders' viewpoints?
2. Which do you think is likely to be most successful in reaching a decision.

6.4 **Lesson 4: Shifting world-views and their contexts**

Views of the world are shifting (Roorda 2007). In 1300 the nobility were elevated above the rest of the populace. In 1700 white people felt superior to other people. In 1900 men were considered to be above women, and in 2000 people were considered more important than animals (see Table 6.1).

Table 6.1 **Shifting views of the world**

1300	1700	1900	2000	2050
Nobility	White people	Men	People	?
Other people	Other people	Other people	Other animals	?

Growing prosperity and well-being enables us to act in a more ethically responsible way. The context is important. Livestock (pigs, cows) can be seen as producers of food, pets or even housemates. If we are willing to pay more for our meat, our view on such animals may improve and shift and they may be seen as pets (or even housemates). People who can afford to pay more for their food are likely to want animals to be treated better and buy meat from free-range chickens or pigs. In addition to cost, religious or other beliefs may play a part, too: consider for example, vegetarians or people who do not eat meat, or the position of cows in India, extolled as sacrosanct partners in society.

A rat may be seen as a pet, a pest, or a laboratory animal. Have you ever thought of a person as a pest? With the current population size, it is beginning to look like it. If humans prove to be a pest, all of a sudden different ethical rules may apply. In 2010 there were devastating floods in Pakistan, the country with the highest population growth, where poverty has contributed to deforestation and building in river beds for lack of space. When there are shortages, communities often move away to new territories, which can result in wars with the existing communities of those territories. What ethics are involved then?

Huib Klamer (2009) points out that, when an environmental protection organisation has an eye only for the interests of the environment, without realising that other values are at stake too, in a sense they become fundamentalists. Entrepreneurs are not by definition bad, just as NGOs are not by definition good (and vice versa). We must go beyond black-and-white thinking, thinking in terms of good and bad. Complacency or always having the last word does not reflect well on anyone and arouses indignation.

Freedom of speech, for example, is an extremely important good, but, when forced to the limit, it may damage people considerably. A value always affects other values, values with which a balance should be found. According to Klamer (2009), one of the keys to finding this balance is the principle Stephen Covey (1989) formulates in *The 7 Habits of Highly Effective People*: 'Seek first to understand, then to be understood.' This requires an attitude of openness, attentive listening, and respect for the person with whom you are communicating. Such dialogue is about mutual acknowledgement of values, interests and the actual facts. That process brings about 'truth', which is nevertheless always relative and remains provisional, and develops into a progressing understanding (just as the classical dialogues by Socrates and Plato were always aimed at finding truth).

Other people's values must always be respected. This requires what Aristotle called the virtue of wisdom, or practical wisdom. Sustainable choices can be made only by involving all concerned parties in the process. It is hardly ever a case of good or bad. One value always affects other values. A sound policy and acting by it means finding a balance between all values at stake at a given time. Compassion is a key word here. Compassion turns an opponent into a human being and it is compassion that can overcome the distinction between 'good' and 'bad'.

7
Summary

7.1 **Chapter 1. Introduction to environmental ethics**

The general goals for the chapter were to understand: the complexity of environmental ethics and basic environmental problems in different media; the scientific developments and the basic philosophical background behind environmental approaches to comprehend how the relationship between human beings and nature is affected and changed in time; and the necessity of harmonising environmental ethics with pollution control and monitoring activities to overcome environmental problems.

The complexity of environmental problems

Environmental problems are growing rapidly and human beings have to face their destructive consequences. These problems have different dimensions that must be considered while trying to solve them (ecological, economic, social, cultural, technical, etc.), making environmental problems complicated and peculiar. Several dilemmas are raised by this multi-dimensional characteristic and this complexity can be confronted only by changing human behaviour towards the environment. It is necessary for people (especially environmental experts as role-models in society and decision-makers as the shapers of environmental policies) to adopt and harmonise ethical dimensions to the scientific, technological, economical, social and legal aspects of controlling environmental pollution to achieve effective environmental protection.

There is a need for a mechanism to replace existing codes of behaviour with a set of values that can be internalised to guide environmental professionals. These environmental ethical values differ from laws by being informal and unwritten values on which to base an individual's conduct towards the environment. Because most environmental problems are anthropogenic in origin, it is very important to understand the sources and impacts of environmental problems in different media (air, water, land, etc.) and how ecosystems function. The 'wholeness' of the ecosystem and the fragility of nature, together with one's position within nature, need to be understood to reach a state of consciousness. Scientific knowledge and experiences of nature increase sensitivity and may lead to facilitated consciousness that leads to a sense of responsibility.

The socio-economic background and environmental responsibility

We are running out of time. We are very close to the end of present consumption habits and living styles; in other words, behaviour is not changing in an environmentally sensitive direction. Some issues occur suddenly and unexpectedly so delays before science catches up may be unavoidable. For example, we don't know when an economic or an ecological crisis will arise, nor do we know the long-term impacts on the environment of some technological developments such as nanotechnology, artificially created lives or the use of biofuels. The moral development of individuals is therefore urgently needed, which means they should form their own ethical framework to live in harmony with nature by assessing the consequences of their relationship with nature. Basic facts about how natural ecosystems function and the technical dimensions of environmental pollution and control practices should be integrated with our judgements on the intrinsic value of nature and our commitments to other living things and to future generations.

The history of environmentalism

In the mechanistic world-view created during the 17th century, scientific revolution constructed the world as a machine made up of interchangeable atomic parts manipulated by humans. Nature was seen as a commodity and instrumental good servings the welfare of human beings. This mechanistic view, the product of early capitalism, lay at the root of many environmental problems but has been replaced, as the world began to experience environmental problems, by an ecocentric world-view that is holistic, emphasising the importance of the whole over the parts, and does not separate humans from the environment. This ecological paradigm entails a new ethic in which all parts of the ecosystem, including humans, are of equal value and recognises the intrinsic value of all beings. It pushes social and ecological systems towards new patterns of production, reproduction and consciousness that will improve the quality of human life and nature.

7.2 **Chapter 2. Environmental ethics: The search for decision criteria**

The general goals for the chapter were: to find a working definition of ethics; to understand three main theories of ethics, the meaning of norm and value and how correct moral reasoning works; to be able to describe, analyse and assess a moral problem and justify the response; and to understand how ethics apply to the environment.

Towards a working definition of ethics

By looking at the history of Greek philosophy to discover the roots of ethics and by confronting ethics with other disciplines it is possible to elicit a working definition of ethics: 'the systematic thinking about the action of humans asking the question whether that action is good or not good in the end'.

That definition leads to normative ethics, which attempts to clarify values by using moral arguments. 'In the end' refers to a conflict of values: ethical problems have to do with a conflict of values. Ethics leads to the questions: What ought I to do? How should I act? What is right in this situation? When I choose, what are my arguments for that choice? Which norm or value is the most important to make that choice? Normative ethics encompasses three main ethical theories: teleological theories, deontological theories, and virtue ethics.

One teleological theory is utilitarianism, first advanced by Bentham and J.S. Mill. Utilitarianism identifies the criterion for the good or bad nature of a human action in the benefit or the harm it causes. The action should benefit not only the actor but also other people involved. An important question is who is involved in a certain action. When the action benefits the majority, it is good; when it harms most of them, it is not good.

Deontological theories don't consider the consequences or goals of the actions. Deontological philosophers argue that an action is right if it is executed according to a principle or norm. The ethical question of what one ought to do is judged by one's intentions and what one considers to be one's duty. The godfather of deontology, Immanuel Kant, said that the only thing that is right is good will, intention. We learn what that good will is when we are confronted with duty. A moral duty is a 'maxim', a moral rule. Maxims precede actions.

Virtue ethics call a human action good when one acts according to a supposed universal set of virtues, although different times and different cultures have different sets of values.

Value can be looked in two ways:

- **Functional or instrumental value.** Something has value because people see it as a tool to realise their goals or ends. It is useful, especially economically useful

- **Intrinsic value.** This value is derived from the end in itself

When you participate in an ethical, moral discussion, correct moral reasoning requires you to make your ethical presupposition clear, agree on the facts of the situation and verify whether any terms employed in your presupposition can be used for the factual situation.

Moral dilemmas

For a dilemma to be classified as moral it has to meet five criteria:

1. You can't avoid the dilemma. You are at a junction and must go left or right. Even when you don't make a choice, you choose

2. Other people are involved

3. Any choice is of interest to those involved and can have consequences for the self-respect or happiness of others

4. You can't satisfy everyone

5. The moral actor is free to choose

Environmental ethics challenges whether the reasons why people's interests have to be taken into consideration are also sufficient to apply to other living beings, elements of nature or even nature as a whole. In professional ethics it is also important to decide whether the moral dilemma is under your personal control. You can only identify, analyse and solve professional moral dilemmas if they are personalistic rather than structural. Moral problems in a professional situation can be dealt with by using a professional code.

Moral quality, when confronted with a moral dilemma in a professional situation, has to do with the action itself and with the procedure. Moral quality can only be reached by compromise—the key word to describe the procedure is 'together'. In a professional situation a step-by-step scheme can be used to describe, analyse and assess a moral dilemma and justify the decision made.

Defining environmental ethics

Environmental ethics is about moral care for nature and the environment. That moral care depends on what is moral status and what has moral status. A definition of environmental ethics is 'systematic thinking about the action of humans towards nature and environment asking the question whether that action is good or not good in the end'.

Nature and environment can have meaning for humans in three ways: as a condition of life, by having intrinsic value, and as a means

of production. When one of the three meanings loses so much quality that a group of people considers it problematic or when people
consider the relation with the environment is disturbed, then an
environmental problem exists. So environmental problems are not
individual but social problems. A situation becomes an environmental problem when we realise that there is a difference between the
desirable and the actual situation. Environmental problems can also
be seen as conflicts of value, which environmental ethics helps to analyse and solve. But what are values and who or what has value?

There are two main groups of value perspectives: the anthropocentric and the non-anthropocentric. The distinction is whether only
human beings have value (anthropocentric) or whether other elements
of nature and environment also have value (non-anthropocentric).
These perspectives are discussed in more detail in Chapter 4.

7.3 **Chapter 3. The challenge to environmental ethics**

The general goal of the chapter was to understand how the field of
environmental ethics is structured, the central areas of environmental ethics, and the essential levels of environmental reasoning.

Three areas of environmental ethics

Environmental ethics is an ethics of application. Its worth depends
on whether moral intrinsic value is attached to the environment—
nature—or not. If it is, we can distinguish three areas of environmental ethics, which together build an ascending sequence. Each
subsequent area includes the former or extends it with an additional
'moral agent':

- **Ethics of resources.** When a value is ascribed to nature only in
  relation to humans, we talk about ethics of resources. Resource
  ethics asks how we can use the raw materials and environmental
  media (such as water and soil) provided by nature without causing irreversible damages (overexploitation or environmental

pollution). Such ethics can be justified solely on anthropocentric grounds: that is, in the interests of people

- **Animal ethics** is concerned with the well-being of individual beings that are sensitive to pain. The term 'animal ethics' is ambiguous as it usually applies only to *sentient* organisms. So animal ethics asks whether animals—at least the ones with sensitivity (to pain)—possess a value and a purpose in themselves. And, if so, it asks what this means in an ethical sense with regard to our relation and behaviour towards them. A consequent animal ethics moves beyond the sole anthropocentric approach by thinking in a 'pathocentric' way

- **Ethics of nature** attends to the moral aspects of dealing with lower 'insentient' life forms (plants, fungi, bacteria, etc.) as well as with other supra-individual biotic entities as species, ecosystems and landscapes. Nature ethics asks whether each form of life or complex natural system—and perhaps even the nature as a whole—possesses moral value and therefore is absolutely worthy of protection. Such ethics (however it might be substantiated) goes—even more than animal ethics—beyond the scope of an environmental ethics that solely respects the interests of humans. Instead of being anthropocentric, nature ethics is physiocentric oriented

Three levels of environmental reasoning

In order to establish a classification of environmental ethics it is important not only to discriminate the three areas of ethics (among environmental ethicists these are largely agreed), but also to distinguish several levels on which environmental ethics are implemented. Three such levels can be outlined:

1. **Philosophical level (ethics).** This 'high' level deals with fundamental explanatory statements: ethical claims of validity are raised, which should be applied universally: that is, for all members of the ethical discourse community

2. **Political–legal level (laws).** This level deals with the definition of collective binding normative regulations and aims

for political actions (e.g. environmental quality goals). Every definition of this kind presupposes certain environmental attitudes and other political decisions made in the past. All relevant environmental aims and programmes are decided and implemented by political organs such as governments, parliaments and public administration

3. **Casuistic level (single cases and actions).** Central to this level are tangible cases of environmental contamination or destruction, responsible methods and measures for the protection or regeneration of a polluted or destructed environment. Primarily, these measures are technical. Practical environmental management is required, and the know-how of environmental experts (environmental engineers, technicians etc.) is central

7.4 **Chapter 4. Main approaches to environmental ethics**

The general goals of the chapter were to understand that environmental ethics: questions the assumed moral supremacy of human beings over members of other species on earth; seeks rational arguments to assign moral status to nature and its non-human elements; and has two views on these matters, the anthropocentric and non-anthropocentric.

Environmental ethics emerged as a new sub-discipline of philosophy in the early 1970s. Until then philosophy had been questioning human actions only towards human beings. Actions towards nature are dealt with in an anthropocentric way. Those actions are good or not good according to how they affect the well-being of humans. Traditional anthropocentrism is challenged by a less narrowly anthropocentric view and by non-anthropocentrism view.

The anthropocentric view

Anthropocentric environmental ethicists view animals, plants, eco-systems and the whole of nature as having only an instrumental value. The only acceptable reason to conserve and cultivate nature is that satisfaction of basic human needs—such as nourishing the body and maintaining health—depends on nature. Reluctance to use natural resources (animals, fossil fuels, minerals, etc.) can be justified only out of consideration for the needs and interests of contemporary humans or of future generations.

However, some more moderate anthropocentrics may concede that at least an aesthetic argument for protecting nature can be add to this instrumental view of nature: they base the need to conserve and cultivate nature on nature's sensual attractions for us, such as the pleasure we take in walking through a forest or swimming in a lake.

The non-anthropocentric view

The non-anthropocentric view has rational arguments for giving moral status to non-human beings, to elements of nature and environment. The concept of intrinsic value is important in understanding non-anthropocentric views. According to the Dutch philosopher Wouter Achterberg environmental ethics tries to expand narrow morality to the relations between human beings and other organisms, beings. Intrinsic value, in the sense of beings and entities having certain essential properties that are intrinsic values (valuable in themselves), can be used to justify that expansion, and the beings deserve moral consideration or moral respect.

The non-anthropocentric view can be represented by four main theories: pathocentrism, biocentrism, ecocentrism and holism. Pathocentrism says that making sentient beings suffer is wrong; creatures that live have moral status. Biocentrism extends concern for individual well-being, arguing for the intrinsic value of organisms; if we can harm the welfare interests of an organism it is morally considerable regardless of whether it has conscious needs or 'feelings'. In ecocentrism the interdependence of the beings and their surroundings gives moral status to an ecosystem and its members. Holism concerns the whole ('Mother Earth'). The elements of the whole, of the ecosystem, are dependent on the well-being of the whole. That is the argument that gives moral status to the whole and its elements.

Each theory has its proponents; each represents a vision within the four kinds of theory related to the important basic ethical theories: utilitarianism and deontology.

Ethical decision-making

Anthropocentric and non-anthropocentric views and the different theories and their representatives are helpful in ethical decision-making. This can be done by using the step-by-step-scheme or the basic attitudes of human beings towards nature and environment.

The step-by-step-scheme can be used to make an ethical decision on, for example, genetic modification of animals for the benefit of humans. First, it is essential to say what your ethical position is. What is your norm? Step 1 involves describing and analysing the situation (and making sure that values and facts are not confused). In Step 2 these facts are analysed, and the proponents of the different theories (Kant, Singer, Regan, etc.) provide help in doing this. Step 3 asks you to justify your decision.

Another way to assess ethical decisions is to use basic attitudes. Six basic attitudes can be categorised as: despot, enlightened despot, steward, partner, participant and unity. The first three are characterised by the view that nature has only instrumental value to human beings, although the steward has some notion of moral care towards nature. With the partner the view that nature has some intrinsic value in itself is introduced. The basic attitudes can be used to decide what one ought to do or to analyse human actions towards nature and environment. In both cases it is possible to change one's attitude towards one that is giving more (or less) intrinsic value to nature and environment.

7.5 **Chapter 5. The need for political and legal regulation**

The general goal of the chapter was an understanding of: how environmental issues can be regulated by law and politics; how environmental ethics can contribute to this task; the principles of political and legal measures; and the instruments that regulate environmental behaviour.

Why we need political–legal regulation

In the 20th century separate environmental legislation was established, taking account of the growing extent of societal intrusion into nature. The more the environment becomes a scarce good, with many competing to utilise it, and natural habitats (and therefore the plants and animals that inhabit them) are increasingly endangered by the expansion of civilisation, the more politics and law are asked to protect nature from exhaustive cultivation, blight and destruction. The mandate for more efficient policies on nature is due not least to growing public ecological awareness and an increasing appreciation of animals and plants for their own sake.

Political–legal regulation is an important tool for the protection of the environment in accordance with economics and social life. It is a complex and interlocking body of statutes, common law, treaties, conventions, regulations and policies that, very broadly, operate to regulate the interaction of humanity with the rest of the biophysical or natural environment. The purpose of all legal rules concerning the protection of environment is to reduce or minimise the impacts of human activity, both on the natural environment for its own sake and on humanity itself.

Principles for political and legal measures

Serious and substantial environmental law has to be guided by some high-ranking principles. For many national regulations in the field of environmental law within the European Union (e.g. in Germany), four basic principles are the basis for all processes of environmental law-making: the precautionary principle, the polluter-pays principle,

the principle of sustainable development (concerning the integration of environmental protection and economic development), and
the cooperation principle.

Regulation of environmental behaviour

To enforce environmental policy principles and objectives two instruments are implemented in the legal framework of many states within
the European Union: (1) different types of environmental planning,
and (2) different measures for regulating environmental behaviour.

Environmental planning is an important means of precautionary protection. Such planning takes place as a multi-stage process,
involving registering the current situation, forecasting future developments and considering conflicting interests. It is an indispensa-
ble instrument of environmental policy because without it particular
environmental goals could not be implemented. Many different societal protagonists (administrative departments, political parties, environmental associations, private stakeholders, etc.) have an interest
in the definition of environmental goals. Environmental protection
associations, in particular, through participation on advisory boards
and representation in the public media, can gain attention. But only
what will be reflected in politically accepted environmental goals
and in applicable environmental law can actually take effect. Environmental ethics will gain practical importance only if public ecological awareness is mobilised, with raised sensitivity to the ethical
relevance of plants, animals or even entire ecosystems, and finds its
expression in definitions of standards in ecological policy and in a
range of measures in public environmental protection programmes.

Environmental behaviour is perhaps the most important objective for environmental policy and education. Instruments to regulate
environmental behaviour can be categorised as direct or indirect.
Direct regulation of behaviour pertains to legal measures designed to
immediately affect environmental behaviour. The 'classical' instrument of this type is environmental regulatory law, which originates
from police and regulatory law and generally punishes non-compli-
ance by imposing sanctions. Indirect regulation of behaviour does
not rely on norms mandating behaviour, but aims to influence motivation: incentives are provided for environmental friendly behaviour

while leaving discretion to the addressee. Indirect instruments include informational measures and economic instruments, such as levies certificates and subsidies.

Eco-political successes, influenced by environment ethical considerations, have so far emerged first and foremost in areas where the problems are very noticeable or have provoked concern (especially in regard to human health). Air and water pollution control are the most important areas within the European Union and OECD countries where such successes have been achieved. In contrast, less immediately noticeable problems—a creeping deterioration of the environment—are scarcely solved: this concerns above all land consumption, loss of biodiversity and the contamination of soil and groundwater with hazardous substances. In the European Union countries increased endeavours and capacities for actions will become necessary in the future.

7.6 Chapter 6. From environmental ethics to sustainable decision-making

The general goals for this chapter were: to understand the principles taken into consideration in sustainable decision-making and how to use the step-by-step tool to help with sustainable decision-making; to be aware of two methods of assessing the competing views of stakeholders and of the effects of changing world-views.

Principles of sustainable development and cradle to cradle

In recent years we have become more aware that environmental issues must be viewed in their entirety. As with all environmental issues, there are social, economic and ecological aspects and a balance must be found in the relationship between people, profit and planet (the three Ps, or the triple bottom line). Furthermore, a proper assessment should take into account the (distant) future and the effects on developing countries.

The cradle-to-cradle principle is receiving increased attention. This concept wants to achieve a new generation of products free from all harmful substances and be fully recyclable. Easily separated degradable materials will enter the biosphere as nutrients, and non-degradable materials the technosphere to be re-used, with all processes using energy from renewable sources. The achievement of this would enable the world to produce whatever it needed for many years to come.

A step-by-step plan for sustainable decision-making

The step-by-step system introduced in earlier chapters can be applied to sustainable decision-making; a sample version might include

Step 1: Description and analysis

- Describe the problem and determine the stakeholders. Analyse their interests with regard to people, profit and planet

Step 2: Assessment

- What solutions might the various stakeholders come up with and what are their pros and cons? What do the solutions have in common?

- What do constitutional principles imply (such as the principle of precautions, the principle of 'the polluter pays' and the principle of good neighbourliness)?

- What do resource ethics, nature ethics and sustainable development ethics say?

- What do the principles of sustainable development (three Ps) and cradle-to-cradle design say?

- Make a decision and reach a compromise

Step 3 Justification

- Can you defend your decision?

- Would people who are considered a great moral example have come to the same decision?

- Had your friends or relatives been affected, would you have come to the same decision or would you mind if the decision affected you personally?

- Is the decision in conflict with your own standards and values? What does your conscience tell you?

- Is the decision in conflict with law and legislation or with the ethics of your profession or company?

Two methods for comparative assessment

To reach an ethical decision, the people, profit and planet arguments of the various stakeholders must be assessed. In a round-table discussion you can exchange arguments against one another, but there is also another method that involves solving **with** one another: the 'six thinking hats'.

Shifting world-views and their contexts

In 1300 nobility were elevated above the rest of the population. In 1700 white people felt superior to others. In 1900 men were considered to be above women and in 2000 people were considered more important than animals. Growing prosperity and well-being enables us to act in a more ethically responsible way and context is important. Perhaps in 2050 there will have been another shift with mammals elevated above other creatures and equal among themselves.

So views on the world shift. One value always affects others and having a sound policy and acting accordingly means finding a balance between all values at stake at a given time. Compassion is the key word here. Compassion turns an opponent into a human being. Compassion can overcome the contrast between 'good' and 'bad', because nobody is all good and nobody all bad.

7.7 **Conclusion and outlook**

It is very clear that environmental problems cannot be solved by technical means alone. Technological approaches have to be integrated and harmonised with the ethical dimensions of problems to find concrete and long-term solutions. To achieve a balance between technology and the ethical dimension, experts should at least have environmental consciousness in addition to their environmental knowledge. This means, for example, in environmental monitoring it will not be enough for environmental experts to know where and how to get samples, how to analyse them and how to evaluate the results; they will also have to understand the function of each part in the ecosystem and its intrinsic value, not just its instrumental value. In other words, they need to understand the internalised ethical values to make them decide and act in a genuinely environment friendly way by feeling that they are part of the environment and feeling nature inside themselves. We can solve environmental problems if, and only if, complete technical information about those problems is supported by ethical insights and environmental awareness. If you have worked your way through this book you will have started down this road.

Annex
The Env-Ethics Project

The Env-Ethics Project arose out of a perceived need, based on some recent efforts and experiences promoted by the European Community, to harmonise environmental knowledge with ethical values to achieve behavioural change and the internalisation of ethical values.

The Sixth Environment Action Programme of the European Community, entitled Environment 2010: Our Future, Our Choice, proposes five priority avenues of strategic action; one of these is empowering people as private citizens and helping them to change behaviour by providing the information they need to make environmentally friendly choices. The United Nations Economic Commission for Europe (UNECE) Convention on Access to Information, Public Participation in Decision-Making and Access to Justice in Environmental Matters (which has been in force since 30 October 2001 and is usually known as the Aarhus Convention) is based on the premise that greater public awareness of, and involvement in, environmental matters will improve environmental protection. The European Commission's Annual Policy Strategy for 2008 (21 February 2007) stressed the renewed Lisbon Strategy for growth and jobs as a major vehicle for promoting a more prosperous, environmentally responsible European Union.

There is a need to increase public sensitivity to environmental and development problems and public involvement in their solutions and to foster a sense of personal environmental responsibility and greater motivation and commitment to environmentally sensitive behaviour.

The Env-Ethics Project therefore aims to train the target group—decision-makers and environmental experts, executives and staff working in municipalities and public and government organisations—both in ethical values to increase environmental awareness and in the technical aspects of pollution control to achieve a clean and healthy environment by applying the main principles of the European Environmental Policy and Integrated Pollution Prevention and Control (IPPC Directive 96/61/EC of 24 September 1996). The development of the technical training part of the training has been completed by the European Commission Leonardo da Vinci Programme Pilot Project MEPC-Training Module for Environmental Pollution Control (RO/02/B/F/PP-141004).

In addition to traditional ways of transferring knowledge, the development of environmental ethics and the adoption of new behaviours are supported by initiatives based on new instruments: for example, communicative tools for information, education and training. New environmental policies and strategies, together with the launch of new fashions and habits in the analysis, appreciation and diffusion of 'best practices', is promoted more widely by means of innovative instruments such as e-learning, vocational training, interactive websites and CD-ROMs.

The aims and objectives of the Env-Ethics Project may be summarised as:

- The development of specific vocational training tools, especially relevant and innovative e-learning content, in the field of environmental pollution control harmonised with environmental ethical values that will be based on the main principles of European environmental policy and the Sixth Environmental Action Plan and renewed Lisbon Strategy, as a major vehicle for promoting an environmentally responsible European Union. It is evident that there is a lack of specific vocational training in the field of environmental ethics for the target groups especially for decision-makers and experts in this field. Technological assistance must be provided to communicate the importance of acting in an environmentally friendly way (obeying unwritten rules) and the latest policies (obeying written rules) in order to have a better and cleaner environment

- The design of final products that will facilitate efficient environmental pollution control by increasing the environmental awareness of individuals and providing educational information about specific cases, best practices, new technologies and current relevant EU legislation in the field of environmental pollution and ethics. A mixed learning methodology (face-to-face and e-learning) will be helpful for everyone to learn about measuring environmental pollution and protection measures. Through training courses target groups will achieve at least four desirable outcomes: increased ethical sensitivity and environmental pollution knowledge; increased knowledge of standards of conduct; improved ethical judgement in environmental controversies; and improved ethical will-power. The project website will support knowledge and information in the communities

- Certification at the end of these vocational training courses that will have validity from vocational and education training (VET) organisations and be helpful to the users in their employment and business

- The successful valorisation of the project among the users

The project will change the target groups' perception of the environment and their attitudes, improving their skills and competences through the products of the project. The e-learning method will facilitate learning and trainees will be able to access the content of the project from any location, thus improving the quality of and access to continuing vocational training. This project will be accessible to everyone, anywhere, through e-learning. E-learning and other products (CD-ROM, book, website, vocational training courses) will cover the latest policies, principles and techniques and will provide technical guidance to decision-makers, executives and staff. The project training tools are the most efficient and technological means of transferring knowledge and new technologies, directives, methods and principles. Apart from this, there is a vast need for vocational training tools for integrating technical knowledge of environmental pollution with environmental ethics. The decision-makers and staff dealing with environmental pollution have few resources for learning the new implementations of the integrated modules and are lacking in environmental awareness. But if the quality of vocational educational training systems and practices is developed according to ethical values and practical methods, it will be much easier to train people, resulting in a cleaner and healthier environment. The training tools will be designed to be practical and cover different environmental ethical cases from each partner country.

Decision-makers should know at least the basic facts about ecology and environmental pollution as well as the threats concerning our habitat in general. Such knowledge should throw light on any misconceptions that may have been the root cause of their apparent lack of concern for the environmental cause and aim to achieve a paradigm shift that would mean basic changes in values and behaviours. The paradigm shift should enable them to have new perceptions based on a biological and holistic world-view rather than on inorganic and mechanistic perspectives. This will be achieved through vocational training of the decision-makers. Similarly environmental staff and experts need to be convinced of why natural protection is important; therefore, in addition to refreshing their technical knowledge on environmental issues, they should be trained on ethical aspects of environment to learn why they are monitoring pollution and why nature is worthy of protection.

Many studies over the past decades have revealed that environmental programmes and projects (e.g. waste management and resource recycling, energy-efficiency, water-resource conservation, pollution control, park and wildlife management, wilderness preservation and biodiversity) have made considerable progress, but there are still many unresolved concerns. Furthermore, in reviewing contemporary studies, it appears that some of the earlier notions and theoretical perspectives for environmental issues are outdated. In order to seek potential solutions to these problems new knowledge and scientific information should be encouraged.

Following this line, the project aims to develop a new training module on environmental ethics that will provide a framework for analysing and evaluating the beliefs and values that underlie environmental controversies that embody ethical dilemmas. Teaching ethics will increase ethical sensibility and ethical will-power (that is, greater ability to act ethically or in a more environmentally friendly way) and thus help to guide the complex decisions that members of the target groups face. They will be challenged to learn skills of critical thinking, writing, speaking and action through the integrated study of technical skills and environmental ethics, learning how to weigh the needs of modern life with the reality of their impact on the natural world. The project will incorporate original case studies from different countries into training modules, helping to emphasise different perceptions of the environment and different strategies that various cultures have employed to resolve ethical dilemmas. Each case will have unique facts, uncertainties and circumstances. This will help to widen the horizon of decision-makers and environmental experts and staff working for the local authorities and governmental organisations that are very effective in shaping environmental policies in Europe and Turkey.

This project will be the first to develop a modular system integrating and harmonising technical aspects of environmental knowledge (by using the products of previous projects) with an ethical background (by using the products of Env-Ethics) in vocational training in Turkey and in Europe. The Env-Ethics Project will develop an ethical background to the previous projects on the transfer of innovation. Thus, this new module will be harmonised and integrated with the products of the completed MEPC-Training Module.

This project will also lead a new approach on the difference between empirical and ethical thinking. These two kinds of thinking are often thought to be the same. But empirical thinking is about how we actually live and act, whereas ethical thinking is about how we *should* live and act. People working in environmental pollution control have no opportunity to undergo such training in the most recent technologies, methods, directives and principles of environmental issues in combination with changing ethical values. Within this perspective, this project will be in the vanguard for subsequent projects leading to the quality assurance of the vocational training in Europe. There is a lack of coordination of environmental education policies on vocational training and no uniform regulatory framework governing how it operates. In addition, there is weakness in the implementation of legislative provisions as a result of insufficient cooperation and collaboration within Europe. Thus this project will both lead a spearhead a new approach to the international standardisation of vocational training programmes and will also improve the standards of members of the target group.

   In order to achieve this, environmental ethics are needed to guide environmental experts and decision-makers in making sound judgements and decisions. Therefore, the most effective impact of this project will be the internalisation of environmental ethics as a forceful tool for the establishment and application of environmentally sound policies and to take appropriate actions as key personnel in environmental protection and pollution control. The project therefore aims at the integration and harmonisation of environmental ethics in pollution control practices to increase the awareness of decision-makers and experts. This will provide a bridge between the 'environmental knowledge' and 'environmental behaviours' of members of the target groups. Env-Ethics project meets the needs of postgraduate and graduate students and vocational education training students and their teachers as well as decision-makers and experts. **Web-link:** www. env-ethics. com/en.

Members of the Env-Ethics Project

- Asst Prof. Dr Gamze Yucel Isildar, Gazi University, Turkey
- Altan Dizdar, Erbil Project Consulting Engineering, Turkey
- Prof. Andrei Florin Danet, University of Bucharest, Romania
- Prof. Dr Jürgen Simon, Hannover Medical School, Germany
- Dr Rainer Paslack, Hannover Medical School, Germany
- Dr Eng. Elmo de Angelis, Training2000, Italy
- Kylene de Angelis, Training2000, Italy
- Rob de Vrind, King William I College, The Netherlands
- Kees Vromans, Hogeschool Hasdenbosch, The Netherlands
- Anouk van Butselaar, King William I College, The Netherlands

- Monika Olsson, Industrial Ecology, Royal Institute of Technology, Sweden
- Damla Baykal, Ministry of Environment and Forestry, Environmental Protection Agency for Special Areas (EPASA), Turkey
- Dr Basak Taseli, Ministry of Environment and Forestry, Environmental Protection Agency for Special Areas (EPASA), Turkey
- Dr Karin Edvardsson Björnberg, Dept of Philosophy and the History of Technology, Royal Institute of Technology, Sweden
- Dr Eng. Daniele Nardi, Macerata, Italy
- Selver Soylu, Fethiye Municipality, Turkey

References and further sources of information

Chapter 1

Botkin, D., and E. Keller (2005) *Environmental Science* (Hoboken, NJ: Wiley, 5th edn).

Carson, R. (1962) *Silent Spring* (Boston, MA: Houghton Mifflin).

Chapman, D. (ed.) (1992) *Water Quality Assessments* (Cambridge, UK: Cambridge University Press).

Ehrlich, P. (1968) *Population Bomb* (Cutchogue, NY: Buccaneer Books).

Ewert, A., and G. Galloway (2004) 'Expressed Environmental Attitudes and Actual Behaviour: Exploring the Concept of Environmentally-Desirable Responses', refereed conference abstract, *10th International Symposium on Society and Resource Management*, Keystone, CO, 2–6 June 2004.

Hardin, G (1968) 'The Tragedy of the Commons', *Science* 162: 1,243-48.

Hardin, G (1974) 'Living on a Lifeboat', *Bioscience*, 24:10; www.garretthardinsociety.org/articles/art_living_on_a_lifeboat.html.

IPCC (Intergovernmental Panel on Climate Change) (2007) *Climate Change 2007: IPCC Fourth Assessment Report; Synthesis Report* (Geneva: IPCC; www.ipcc.ch/publications_and_data/ar4/syr/en/spms2.html, accessed 25 March 2012).

Klare, M. (2008) 'The Crisis and the Environment', *Global Policy Forum*; www.globalpolicy.org/social-and-economic-policy/the-environment/general-analysis-on-the-environment/44082.html, accessed 25 March 2012.

Leopold A. (1949) 'The Land Ethic', in *A Sand County Almanac* (New York: Oxford University Press).

Marsh, W., and J. Grossa (2005) *Environmental Geography: Science, Landuse and Earth Systems* (Hoboken, NJ: John Wiley).

Meadows. D.H., D.L. Meadows, J. Randers and W.W. Behrens III (1972) *The Limits to Growth* (New York: Universe Books).

Merchant, C. (1992) *Radical Ecology* (New York/London: Routledge).

Olli, E., G. Grendstadt and D. Wollebaek (2001) 'Correlates of Environmental Behaviors: Bringing Back Social Context', *Environment and Behavior* 33: 181-208.

Pepper, D. (1996) *Modern Environmentalism* (London/New York: Routledge).

Raven, P., and L. Berg (2006): *Environment* (Hoboken, NJ: John Wiley, 5th edn).

Ray, B.T. (1995) *Environmental Engineering* (Boston, MA: PWS).

Simonnet, D. (1982), *L'écologisme* (Paris: PUF).

Stocks, K., and S. Albrecht (1993) 'Ethical Dilemmas: The Ethical Environment'; findarticles.com/p/articles/mi_m4153/is_n3_v50/ai_14535031, accessed 25 March 2012.

US Climate Change Strategic Program (2003) *Strategic Plan for the US Climate Change Science Program* (Washington DC: Climate Change Strategic Program; Chapter 6 available at www.climatescience.gov/Library/stratplan2003/final/ ccspstratplan2003-chap6. pdf, accessed 25 March 2012).

Sutherland, W., *et al.* (2008) 'Future Novel Threats and Opportunities Facing UK Biodiversity Identified by Horizon Scanning', *Journal of Applied Ecology* 45.3: 821-33.

Tekeli, İ. (2000) 'Türkiye Çevre Tarihçiliğine Açılırken', in Z. Boratav (ed.), *Türkiye'de çevrenin ve çevre korumanın tarihi sempozyumu* (İstanbul: Türk Tarih Vakfı Yayınları).

Vesilind, A., and S. Morgan (2004) *Introduction to Environmental Engineering* (Pacific Grove, CA: Brooks Cole, 2nd edn).

WCED (World Commission on Environment and Development) (1987) *Our Common Future* (also known as the Brundtland Report; New York: WCED).

Chapter 2

Achterberg, W (1994) *Een inleiding in de Milieufilosofie, samenleving, natuur en duurzaamheid* (Assen, The Netherlands: Van Gorcum): 4-5.

Beauchamp, T.L. (2001) *Philosophical Ethics: An Introduction to Moral Philosophy* (New York: McGraw-Hill, 3rd edn).

Meykamp, W.J.M., P.T. Westerhuis and S.A. Terpstra (1989) *Sociale Ethiek: Basisboek* (Groningen, The Netherlands: Walters-Noordhof).

Van Ast, J.A., and H. Geerlings (1993) *Milieukunde & milieubeleid: Een introductie* (Alphen aan den Rijn, The Netherlands: Samson/H.D. Tjeenk Willink).

Van Hilhorst, M.T. (1989) 'Niet voor alles verantwoordelijk; Alles heeft zijn uur: Op zoek naar een specifieke beroepsethiek', in D.G.A. Koelega (ed.), *De ingenieur buitenspel? Over de maatschappelijke verantwoordelijkheid in technische en natuurwetenschappelijke beroepen* (Gravenhage, The Netherlands: Uitgeverij Boekencentrum): 110-26.

Van Willigenburg, T., A. van den Beld, F.R. Heeger and M.F. Verweij (1993) *Ethiek in praktijk* (Assen, The Netherlands: van Gorcum): 32-36.

Further reading and sources of information

Billington, R. (2003) *Living Philosophy: An Introduction to Moral Thought* (New York: Routledge, 3rd edn).

Blackburn, S. (2001) *Being Good: A Short Introduction to Ethics* (Oxford: Oxford University Press).

De Jong, F.J., and W. Leendertz (1976) *Beknopte inleiding in de ethiek* (Deventer, The Netherlands: Van Loghum Slaterus).

De Leeuw, J. (1995) *Handel-Wijs; levensbeschouwelijke vorming en bedrijfsethiek voor MBO, sector economie* (Best, The Netherlands: Damon).

Fretz, L. (1980) *Ethiek als wetenschap, een kritische inleiding in de filosofische ethiek* (Meppel, The Netherlands: Boom).

Hubbeling, H.G., *et al.* (1985) *Ethiek in meervoud* (Assen, The Netherlands: Van Gorcum).

Jeuken, M. (1977) *Ethiek* (Assen, The Netherlands: Van Gorcum).

Panza, C., and A. Potthast (2010) *Ethics for Dummies* (Indianapolis, IN: Wiley).

Segers, L. (1992) 'Waarover gaat ethiek?', *Verbum* 56.5: 98-101.

Van Eijck, J. (1984) *Filosofie, een inleiding* (Meppel, The Netherlands: Boom).

Van Willigenburg, T., G. den Hartog and F. Jacobs (2011) *Inleiding Ethiek* (Maastricht, The Netherlands: Boekenplan).

Willemse, H. (ed.) (1992) *Woordenboek filosofie*. (Assen/Maastricht, The Netherlands: Van Gorcum).

Websites for further information and resources

Stanford Encyclopaedia of Philosophy (SEP): plato.stanford.edu; plato.stanford.edu/entries/ethics-environmental

www.freedomainradio.com/videos.html (video and radio on philosophy and ethics)

www.philosophytalk.org (weekly talks from 13 January 2004)

www.angelfire.com/ego/philosophyradio

www.philosophypathways.com/programs/pak5.html (includes introductory booklist)

www.ethicsweb.ca/resources

www.ethicsweb.ca/guide

www.scu.edu/ethics/practicing/decision/thinking.html

www.scu.edu/ethics/practicing/decision/framework.html

www.ethicsscoreboard.com/rb_5step.html

www.ethics.org/resources/articles-organizational-ethics.asp?aid=940

www.criticalthinking.net/index.html

www.bbc.co.uk/ethics/introduction/intro_1.shtml

www.bbc.co.uk/ethics/introduction/endinitself.shtml

publicethicsradio.org

www.youtube.com/watch?v=7--Nnyq3lOI

ethics.sandiego.edu/theories/Intro/index.asp

www.isanet.org/int_ethics_books (bibliography of new books)

Chapter 3

Brecht, B. (1961) 'Anecdotes of Mr Keuner', in *Tales from the Calendar* (trans. Y. Kapp and M. Hamberger of *Kalendergeschichten*; London: Methuen).

Eser, U., and T. Potthast (1999) *Naturschutzethik: Eine Einführung für die Praxis* (Baden-Baden: Nomos).

Krebs, A. (1999) *Ethics of Nature* (Berlin: De Gruyter).

Ott, K. (2000) 'Umweltethik: Einige vorläufige Positionsbestimmungen', in K. Ott and M. Gorke (eds.), *Spektrum der Umweltethik* (Marburg, Germany: Metropolis): 13-39.

Thomas, K. (1983) *Man and the Natural World: A History of Modern Sensibility* (New York: Pantheon).

Von der Pfordten, D. (1996) *Ökologische Ethik* (Reinbek, Germany: Rowohlt).

Chapter 4

Achterberg, W. (1994) *Samenleving, Natuur en Duurzaamheid, een inleiding in de milieufilosofie* (Assen, The Netherlands: Van Gorcum).

Attfield, R. (2003) *Environmental Ethics: An Overview for the Twenty-first Century* (Cambridge, UK: Polity Press).

Barry, B. (1999) 'Sustainability and Intergenerational Justice', in A. Dobson (ed.), *Fairness and Futurity* (Oxford: Oxford University Press): 93-117.

Cochrane, A. (2007) 'Environmental Ethics', in J. Fieser and B. Dowden (general eds.), *Internet Encyclopedia of Philosophy* (www.iep.utm.edu/envi-eth).

Gewirth, A. (2001) 'Human Rights and Future Generations', in M. Boylan (ed.), *Environmental Ethics* (Upper Saddle River, NJ: Prentice Hall): 207-11.

Hettinger, N. (2005) 'Tom Regan: Case for Animal Rights'; spinner.cofc.edu/hettinger/Environmental_Ethics/Regan_Case_For_Animal_Rights.htm, accessed 25 March 2012.

Kockelkoren, P.J.H. (1993) *Van een plantaardig naar een plantwaardig bestaan: Ethische aspecten van biotechnologie bij planten* (Enschede, The Netherlands: Universiteit van Twente).

Krebs, A. (1999) *Ethics of Nature: A Map* (Berlin: De Gruyter).

Leopold, A. (1949) *A. Sand County Almanac* (Oxford, Oxford University Press)

Palmer, C. (2008) 'An Overview of Environmental Ethics', in A. Light and H. Rolston III (eds.), *Environmental Ethics: An Anthology* (Malden, MA: Blackwell): 15-37.

Parfit, D.(1984) *Reasons and Persons* (Oxford: Clarendon Press).

Regan, T. (1983) *The Case for Animal Rights* (London: Routledge).

Routley, R., and V. Routley (1979) 'Human Chauvinism and Environmental Ethics', in D. Mannison *et al.* (eds.), *Environmental Philosophy* (Canberra: Australian National University): 96-198.

Singer, P. (1975) *Animal Liberation: A New Ethics for Our Treatment of Animals* (New York: HarperCollins).

Singer, P. (1993) *Practical Ethics* (Cambridge: Cambridge University Press, 2nd edn).

Taylor, P.W. (1986) *Respect for Nature: A Theory of Environmental Ethics* (Princeton, NJ: Princeton University Press).

Wenz, P.S. (2001) *Environmental Ethics Today* (New York/Oxford: Oxford University Press).

White, L.T., Jr (1967) 'The Historical Roots of Our Ecologic Crisis', *Science* 155.3767 (10 March 1967): 1,203-207.

WCED (World Commission on Environment and Development) (1987) *Our Common Future* (also known as the Brundtland Report; New York: WCED; www.un-documents.net/wced-ocf.htm, accessed 25 March 2012).

Zweers, W. (1994) 'Milieufilosofie', in J.J. Boersema (ed.), *Basisboek Milieukunde* (Meppel, The Netherlands: Boom): 326-40.

Zweers, W. (1995) *Participeren aan de Natuur* (Utrecht, The Netherlands: Van Arkel).

Zweers, W. (2000) *Participating with Nature* (trans. J. Taylor; Utrecht, The Netherlands: International Books).

Further reading and sources of information

Düwell, M. (2006) *Handbuch Ethik* (Stuttgart-Weimar: Verlag J.B. Metzler).

Kuipers, K. (2004) 'Filosofie en duurzame ontwikkeling, filosofieonderwijs rond een maatschappelijk vraagstuk', DHO; www.dho.nl, publicaties, vakreviews.

Royakkers, L., I. van de Poel and A. Pieters (eds.) (2004) *Ethiek & Techniek, morele overwegingen in de ingenieurspraktijk* (Baarn, The Netherlands: HBuitgevers).

Vesilind, P.A., and A.S. Gunn. (1998) *Engineering, Ethics and Environment* (Cambridge, UK: Cambridge University Press).

Zimmermann, M.E., *et al.* (2004) *Environmental Philosophy: From Animal Rights to Radical Ecology* (Upper Saddle River, NJ: Prentice Hall, 4th edn).

Websites

Encyclopedias and overviews (search environmental ethics, intrinsic values and individual names)

plato.stanford.edu

ethics.sandiego.edu

www.cep.unt.edu

www.cep.unt.edu/anthol.html

spinner.cofc.edu/hettinger

www.utilitarian.net/singer

www.tomregan-animalrights.com

Chapter 5

Commission of the European Communities (2000) *Communication from the Commission on the Precautionary Principle.* (COM[2000]1 final, 2 February 2000; Brussels: Commission of the European Communities).

German Federal Government (1976) *Report on the Environment* (BT-Drs. 7/5684: Bonn: German Federal Government).

Daly, H.E. (1973) *Towards a Steady State Economy* (San Francisco: Freeman).

Daly, H.E. (1991) *Steady-State Economics* (Washington, DC: Island Press; 2nd edn).

Dyllick, T., and K. Hockerts (2002) 'Beyond the Business Case for Corporate Sustainability', *Business Strategy and the Environment* 11.2: 130-41.

Knopp, L. (2008) *International and European Environmental Law with Reference to German Environmental Law* (Berlin: Lexxion Verlagsgesellschaft).

Meadows, D.H., D.L. Meadows, J. Randers and W.W. Behrens III (1972) *The Limits to Growth* (New York: Universe Books).

Müller, F. (2005) *Kyoto's Grandfathering Principle as an Obstacle to be Overcome* (Working Paper of Research Unit on Global Issues; Berlin: Stiftung Wissenschaft und Politik [German Institute for International and Security Affairs]).

Raffensperger, C., and J. Tickner (eds.) (1999) *Protecting Public Health and the Environment: Implementing the Precautionary Principle* (Washington, DC: Island Press).

Sandin, P., M. Peterson, S.O. Hansson, C. Ruden and A. Juthe (2002) 'Five Charges against the Precautionary Principle', *Journal of Risk Research* 5.4: 287-99.

Simonis, U.E. (ed.) (2003) *ÖkoLexikon* (München: Verlag C.H. Beck).

Stivers, R. (1976) *The Sustainable Society: Ethics and Economic Growth* (Philadelphia, PA: Westminster Press).

United Nations (1987) *Report of the World Commission on Environment and Development* (General Assembly Resolution 42/187 11 December 1987; New York: United Nations; www.un.org/documents/ga/res/42/ares42-187.htm, accessed 25 March 2012).

Van den Belt, H. (2003) 'Debating the Precautionary Principle: "Guilty until Proven Innocent" or "Innocent until Proven Guilty"?', *Plant Physiology* 132: 1,122-26.

Chapter 6

Covey, S (1989) *The 7 Habits Of Highly Effective People* (New York: Free Press).

De Bono, E (1985) *Six Thinking Hats: An Essential Approach to Business Management* (New York: Little, Brown).

Klamer, H. (2009) 'Goed en fout', *P+ Magazine*, January–February 2009; www.duurzaammbo.nl/DuurzaamMBO/DuurzaamMBO/Basismodule/essay.pdf, accessed 13 March 2012.

McDonough, W., and M. Braungart (2002) *Cradle to Cradle* (New York: North Point Press).

Roorda, N. (2006) *Basisboek duurzame ontwikkeling* (Groningen, The Netherlands: Wolters-Noordhoff).

Roorda, N. (2007) *Werken aan duurzame ontwikkeling* (Groningen, The Netherlands: Wolters-Noordhoff).

Van den Herik, K., and P. Winkler (2009) MVO en duurzaam ondernemen (Leeuwarden: The Netherlands: Eisma Edumedia).

About the editors

Kees Vromans is a lecturer in the Department of Environmental Studies at HAS Den Bosch, a university for applied studies on animal, plant, nature and environment, where he has worked since 1983. The scope of the department has evolved towards sustainable development. After social work and working as a pastor, he studied philosophy, especially environmental ethics. He developed four modules based on the ideas of his professors Wouter Achterberg and Wim Zweers. The main goal of his work with students is clarifying values. Other fields of interest are sustainable development and internationalisation, the last inspired by the adoption of two girls from Guatemala. A back-to-the-roots trip in 2002 started a new never-ending journey: sustainable solutions worldwide. The next step is reflection on sustainable development using the 'tools' of environmental ethics. Kees is holder of a Working and Learning for Sustainable Development (WLSD) award; in 2003 he was winner of the Egg of Columbus, an award for sustainability and innovation by seven Dutch ministries; and in 2006 was nominated for the Sustainable Education in the Tropics (SET) award.

Gamze Isildar is an Assistant Professor at Gazi University, Turkey. She is an environmental engineer with a PhD in the field of environmental ethics. She teaches courses in pollution monitoring and control, environmental policies and legislation, environmental philosophy and ethics, and principles of environmental engineering. She has coordinated several national and international projects. Her areas of interest are environmental ethics, environmental policies, environmental training and public awareness, preparation of environmental management plans for sensitive zones, water quality and sustainable cities and campuses.

Rainer Paslack is a German sociologist, philosopher and human biologist. The main areas of his academic interests are bioethics, environmental ethics and technology assessment in gene technology, biomedicine and eco-sciences. From 1980 to 1994 he was a research assistant at the Institute for the History of Science and Technology of the University of Bielefeld; since 1994 he has been the Research Director of the Department of Technology Assessment at the Corporation for Innovation and Technology Transfer in Biomedicine (GBM) in Bad Oeynhausen (Germany). He has written several books and many articles about biotechnology, the history of science, and environmental ethics and is co-editor of the book series Medicine, Technology and Society.

Jürgen Walter Simon is a German lawyer and economist. The main areas of his academic interest are medical law, biotechnology law, economic law and environmental law. Since 1989 he has been a professor at the Leuphana University Lüneburg; he is a member of the Centre for Ethics and Law in the Life Sciences (CELLS) at the Medical University Hannover and Visiting Scholar at the University of London. He is also the Managing Director of the Academy of Finance, Insurance and Law (Hamburg). He has organised or been project partner for many international and national projects all over the world. He is the author of many books and articles, a series editor and co-editor and a member of the advisory board of academic journals.

Rob de Vrind is a Dutch biologist. After graduating from the University of Nijmegen he was a teacher of biology and health studies for 17 years and then worked as sustainability manager at the King William I College in 's-Hertogenbosch, The Netherlands. He been involved in many European projects, including Integral Care Systems, Curriculum Greening Europe, Enersol (solar energy), Zu Hause (hydrogen technology), Environmental Ethics, Cradle to Cradle, Our Common Future). He is the founder and chair of Sustainable Vocational Education and Training in the Netherlands and has lectured in Thailand, the USA and Canada. In 2009 he received the sustainability award from the province of Brabant and in 2011 the Prins Bernard Foundation culture and nature award.

Index